WORLD WAR II
IN
CARTOONS

WORLD WAR II
IN
CARTOONS

Mark Bryant

GRUB STREET • LONDON

For Robert and Julius

First published in hardback 2005 by
Grub Street
4 Rainham Close
London
SW11 6SS

This paperback edition published 2014
Text and picture selection © Mark Bryant 1989

A CIP catalogue record for this book is available from the British Library

ISBN 978-1-909808-11-9

Printed and bound in India by Replika Press Pvt. Ltd.

Front cover: Image by Karl Arnold, taken from *Simplicissimus*, 15 May 1932;
Back cover: Cartoon of Pilot Officer Prune by Bill (Raff) Hooper, 1943

CONTENTS

PREFACE

A picture paints a thousand words, it is said, but – to paraphrase the eminent journalist James Cameron – it does rather depend on who draws the pictures and who writes the words.

This book is intended primarily as a pictorial history of World War II as seen through the eyes of its cartoonists on the spot. Where necessary I have filled out a little historical background to link the images for those, like myself, who were not there, but overall the cartoons tell the story. As far as possible, given the limitations of time and cost, I have tried to gather material from both sides of the conflict but, perhaps surprisingly fifty years after the event, still found considerable sensitivity in this area by business and government archive departments, both at home and abroad. I am also disappointed that a change in their policy has meant that some material from Walt Disney and the *Beano* has had to be omitted though previously published elsewhere.

The main emphasis of this book is on cartoons in newspapers and magazines, though sample material from books, comic strips, animation, aerial leaflets, posters, bomber nose-art etc has also been included. I am also especially pleased to be able to reproduce here for the first time a number of hitherto unpublished cartoons drawn in prisoner-of-war camps.

In the preparation of this book I am indebted to Jane Laslett, Adrian Gilbert and Mandy Little of Bison Books; Alan Gooch and Simon Bucnanan of Design 23; Jenny Wood of the Imperial War Museum; Liz Ottaway and Professor Colin Seymour-Ure of the Centre for the Study of Cartoons and Caricature at the University of Kent at Canterbury; Amanda Jane Doran of *Punch*; the British Library; the British Newspaper Library; the Wiener Library; the Goethe Institute; the Institut Français; the Society for Cultural Relations with the USSR; and the Italian Cultural Institute.

Mark Bryant
London

'At one stroke ... people will understand a pictorial presentation of something which it would take them a long and laborious effort of reading to understand.'

Adolf Hitler

Mein Kampf, Book II, Chapter VI

INTRODUCTION

'Nothing to touch the glory of the great cartoonists! They catch the spirit of the age and then leave their own imprint on it: they create political heroes and villains in their own image; they teach the historians their trade . . . and have proprietors and editors at their mercy.' Michael Foot's words are particularly poignant when applied to the work of cartoonists in World War II, and it may be difficult for generations brought up on a diet of Disney, Superman and 'Peanuts' to realize the immense impact of cartoon art in pre-TV days when the only visual sources of information were cinema newsreels, posters, newspapers and books – all largely black and white. To a news-hungry public, anxious about world affairs, the radio was a lifeline, but it was the political cartoon with its immediacy and universal accessibility – even to the barely literate – that could speak the message mere words could never convey. The propagandists and media manipulators were swift to recognize this power, and as a measure of the regard the cartoonists were held in it is perhaps sufficient to note that the Soviet artist Boris Efimov was reputed to earn more than four times Stalin's salary, Sidney Strube of the *Express* was paid £10,000 a year in the 1930s and a single drawing by Philip Zec in the *Daily Mirror* – one of the highest-selling national dailies in the UK at the time – was debated heatedly in the House of Commons in 1942 and very nearly led to the paper's closure.

The word 'cartoon' (from the Italian for a large sheet of paper or card) was originally applied solely to describe designs for tapestries, mosaics or fresco paintings, but its more widely used modern sense derives from a *Punch* spoof by Leech on a competition inviting designs for decorating the walls of the new Houses of Parliament in 1843. Thereafter, the main weekly full-page topical drawing of the magazine – formerly headed 'Mr Punch's Pencillings' – was referred to as 'the Cartoon' and the word gradually came to be applied to comic drawings generally. Such graphic lampoonery, of course, dates back much further – indeed there is even an early caricature (from another Italian word meaning to overburden or exaggerate) of Tutankhamun's father-in-law, King Akhenaton of Egypt – and the work of Hogarth, Gillray, Rowlandson and Cruikshank all bear witness to the style. However, it was with the arrival, in the nineteenth century, of specialist journals containing cartoons (formerly only available as prints or originals) that their impact really began to be felt. *La Caricature* (1830) and *Le Charivari* (1832) in France, *Punch* (1841) and *Vanity Fair* (1868) in England, *Kladderadatsch* (1848) and *Simplicissimus* (1896) in Germany, and *Puck* (1876) and *Judge* (1881) in the United States, among many others, all published cartoons regularly, and in 1890 Francis Carruthers Gould joined the *Pall Mall Gazette* as the first ever daily newspaper cartoonist. This was the period of Tenniel, Doré, Nast, Du Maurier, Leech, Beerbohm, 'Ape', 'Spy', 'Caran D'Ache', Sambourne, Phil May and Daumier (who was actually imprisoned for a drawing of King Louis Philippe as Gargantua). The twentieth century brought World War I and a new school of raw, biting satire at the hands of Louis Raemakers, Will Dyson, Bruce Bairnsfather, Karl Arnold and Th Th Heine followed by the launch of *Le canard enchaîné* (1915), *Krokodil* (1922), the *New Yorker* (1925) and *Lilliput* (1937). The 1920s and 30s also brought George Grosz and H M Bateman into the spotlight and, already head and shoulders above anyone else in his field, a young David Low who, in Arnold Bennett's words, could draw as fish swim.

The early years of the century also saw the beginnings of a slow transformation in cartoon conventions. National symbols such as Britannia, Germania and Columbia; John Bull, Uncle Sam and Marianne; the British lion, Soviet bear, French cockerel etc – so beloved of the Tenniel school – gradually gave way to caricatures of heads of state and such graphic devices as the swastika, fasces, hammer and sickle, and rising sun. And with the gradual departure of the heroic figures there emerged a series of smaller character types: Bairnsfather's Old Bill, Strube's John Citizen, Mauldin's Willie and Joe, Low's Colonel Blimp, Jon's Two Types and Breger's GI Joe. Animal images persisted, but on the whole (apart from Churchill as a bulldog) these were mainly of the basest kind by the outbreak of World War II – curs, alleycats, wolves, toads, rats, sharks, spiders, snakes, bats, octopi – and usually with a politician's head. The national leaders themselves were a gift to caricaturists with such ready-made identity 'tabs' as Hitler's Chaplinesque moustache, Goering's girth and unusual uniforms, Churchill's cigar and (in Axis pictures) whisky bottle, Stalin's pipe and drooping moustache, and Roosevelt's cigarette-holder and walking-stick.

The pressures and constraints of wartime brought their own problems for cartoonists. Woodpulp shortages in Britain reduced many daily newspapers to four pages; dissident and Jewish cartoonists in Europe were interned or fled the Nazi regimes; censorship on both sides hampered creativity; and for Fleet Street staffers in London during the Blitz there was a strong possibility that their drawing-boards might be buried under tons of rubble when they arrived for work. But every cloud had a silver (albeit perhaps ersatz metal) lining: the fight for cartoon space led directly to Osbert Lancaster's development of the one-column 'pocket' cartoon; Nazi purges gave to the Allies Vicky, Szyk, Hoffmeister, Flatter, Steinberg, Trier and other brilliant cartoonists. And the war itself produced countless opportunities for gags: V-weapons, gasmasks, blackout, barrage balloons, the Home Guard, rationing, bomb-shelters, 'business as usual' etc.

As well as the already established staffers and freelancers who adapted their styles to the crisis, a considerable number of cartoonists also emerged from the ranks during the war, notable amongst them being David Langdon (RAF), 'Raff' (RAF), Bill Mauldin (US Army), Dave Breger (US Army), Ronald Searle (Royal Engineers), Ian Fenwick (SAS), 'Paul Crum' (Commando), John Musgrave-Wood (Chindit) and 'Jon' (Eighth Army). At least two were killed in action – Roger Pettiward ('Paul Crum') at Dieppe in 1942 and Ian Fenwick in 1944 – and the war years also claimed the lives of Bernard Partridge (1945), Heath Robinson (1944), Charles Dana Gibson (1944), 'Pont' (1940) and, by suicide, Goebbels' favorite cartoonist, Erich Schilling (1945).

And what of the journals of the Tripartite Pact countries? Julius Streicher's anti-Semitic *Der Stürmer* was illustrated with equal virulence by Fips, the clear line of Pouwels caught the SS viewpoint in the Dutch SS newspaper *Storm SS*, Bogner featured regularly in *Das Schwarze Korps*, and the remaining stars of *Simplicissimus* and *Kladderadatsch*, once violently anti-Hitler (and both finally closed down in 1944) were Erich Schilling and Arthur Johnson respectively. In Italy, *Bertoldo, Marc' Aurelio* and *Il*

420 led the field with cartoonists such as Barbara, Buriko and Giovanni Guareschi (later to be better known for his 'Don Camillo' stories). And in the 'Greater East Asia Co-prosperity Sphere' the official Japanese satirical magazine, *Manga*, featured covers by Hidezo Kondo.

I have concentrated mainly on newspaper and magazine cartoons in this graphic scrapbook of World War II for the simple reason that these would have been the most widely available to the general public. However, the impact of the posters of Fougasse (UK), Gino Boccasile (Italy) and the Kukryniksi group (USSR) amongst others should not be underestimated, particularly as these had the added force of color imagery. Also a number of propaganda animated films were made by the big studios on both sides during the conflict, notable examples being the Donald Duck film *Der Führer's Face* which won an Oscar for Walt Disney in 1942 and Tex Avery's version of the Three Little Pigs story, *The Blitz Wolf*, in the same year (with Hitler as the Big Bad Wolf). Children's comics also reflected the mood of the adult publications, *Beano* running a strip entitled 'Musso the Wop' from December 1941 and *Speed Comics* in the USA showing various 'superheroes' battling with the dictators, for example.

As to the mood of the cartoons themselves throughout the conflict, it is interesting to examine the attitudes of the artists to their subjects. An idea Fougasse put forward in his book *The Good-Tempered Pencil* (1956) was that humor must be essentially kindly, the pencil *must* be good-tempered. Low, to some extent, agreed with this – 'malice clouds the judgement' – and his dictators are more ridiculous than loathsome, while Strube, described by Baldwin as 'a gentle genius', depicts them largely as mistaken persons rather than devilish madmen. By contrast Dyson swore never to draw a line that didn't show war as 'the filthy business it is' and Kondo's fanged Roosevelt, Fips' poisonous-looking Jews, Bert's vicious anti-Nazi drawings and the many slavering figures in the work of the Russian cartoonists take a completely different stance. *Schadenfreude* or a jolly joke? Pulitzer prize-winning cartoonist Bill Mauldin once described the cartoonist's job as being to 'circle and stab, circle and stab.' On this criterion it would seem that both views can be held – some cartoonists just stab more often and more deeply than others.

By its very nature cartoon art is ephemeral. As Osbert Lancaster pointed out in *Signs of the Times* (1961): 'A professional preoccupation with the topical is the surest passport to oblivion, and nothing, not even women's hair-styles, nor the music of the late Ivor Novello, dates as quickly as the apt comment.' Added to which the very medium in which cartoons appear is condemned to the waste-basket by sundown. Apart from Low, Vicky, Strube, Pont, Lancaster, and a very few others who managed to cajole hard-pressed publishers to produce collections of their work, precious little survives today. Hence the present compendium which may, I hope, preserve a few scraps for posterity.

In conclusion, to return to the opening quotation of this Introduction, it is interesting to find from the other side of the fence, as it were, the eminent historian of World War II, A J P Taylor, saying that 'even today historians often give the impression of repeating Low.' Such has been the impact of cartoon art on the narration of history.

PRE-WAR

It is now generally accepted that the seeds of World War II were already planted in the ruins of 1918. By the Treaty of Versailles, signed in June of the following year, the Allies forced a broken Germany to surrender territory and demanded huge reparations. The German economy failed to recover from the war and such was the state of inflation that the Mark, which had stood at four to the dollar in 1918, had reached 130,000 million to the dollar by November 1923. Not unnaturally, Germany began to default on reparations repayments and, in lieu of cash, France and Belgium occupied the Ruhr industrial area.

It was in the climate of discontent generated by these events that a young Austrian ex-soldier, twice decorated with the Iron Cross in the Great War, first made his name in politics. Adolf Hitler (born 20 April 1889) joined the Munich branch of the German Workers' Party (DAP) in September 1919 and by July 1921 had become its leader, changing its title to the National Socialist German Workers' Party – the Nazis. After the Franco-Belgian occupation of the Ruhr district, Hitler attempted to seize power in Bavaria, in imitation of Benito Mussolini's successful 'March on Rome' the previous year. Hitler's Munich *Putsch* failed, however, and he was sentenced to four years' imprisonment in April 1924. During his incarceration at Landsberg he wrote the influential account of his life and philosophy, *Mein Kampf* (My Struggle).

Released from prison after only 13 months, Hitler returned to politics, but he was singularly unsuccessful until the Wall Street Crash of October 1929 threw the world economy into Depression, Germany was hit by mass unemployment and political extremism came back into fashion. In the 1930 German elections the Nazis received 20 percent of the vote. Backed by powerful capitalists and a disillusioned general public, willing to accept the ready scapegoats of Communism, Judaism and the betrayal at Versailles as an explanation for their current ills, the Nazis eventually became the single largest party in Germany. Hitler was appointed Chancellor on 30 January 1933 and a year later, on the death of President Hindenburg, he assumed total power as Führer of the Third Reich.

Having eliminated fractious elements amongst his own supporters in the Night of the Long Knives on 30 June 1934, Hitler swiftly put his theories into practice and began seeking *Lebensraum* (living space) for the German-speaking peoples. He also embarked on rapid rearmament in direct defiance of the terms of the Versailles Treaty. He sent troops into the demilitarized Rhineland in March 1936 and annexed Austria two years later. The British Prime Minister Neville Chamberlain decided that only a policy of appeasement could save Europe from war. At the Munich Conference in September 1938, Chamberlain forced Czechoslovakia to accede to Hitler's demands and hand over the Sudetenland to Germany. Hitler soon carved up the rest of the Czech state, with Poland and Hungary also taking shares. But his next move, against Poland in September 1939, proved the final straw for Britain and France.

Meanwhile, right-wing militarism had also been on the march elsewhere in the world. In Italy, the former socialist editor of *Il Popolo d'Italia*, Benito Mussolini, had merged his anti-Communist groups of followers into the Fascist Party in 1919. In a period of extreme civil unrest, Mussolini put pressure on the government and was appointed prime minister in October 1922 by King Victor Emmanuel III. He rapidly extended his power to become sole dictator (Il Duce) and began to follow an aggressive foreign policy, invading Abyssinia in 1935 and forming a loose collaboration, the 'Axis', with Germany the following year. When a right-wing revolt occurred in Spain in 1936, headed by General Francisco Franco, both Mussolini and Hitler gave active support to the rebellion which eventually toppled the democratically elected Popular Front government.

In the Far East too, there had been unrest in the postwar period. Incensed by arms limitations imposed on them by western treaties and lacking natural resources Japanese militarists agitated for change. In 1931 an incident in Manchuria provided an excuse for a full-scale invasion of the province and by 1938, as a result of the ensuing Sino-Japanese War, Japan controlled all the major Chinese ports.

It was against this background of right-wing dictatorship and rampant militarism that the global conflagration now known as World War II started.

PEACE AND FUTURE CANNON FODDER

The Tiger: 'Curious! I seem to hear a child weeping!'
Will Dyson, *Daily Herald*, 13 May 1919

Vains efforts
Je suis partout, 18 September 1933

In this famous cartoon by the renowned Australian-born artist Will Dyson (1880-1938), the scene is set outside Versailles after the peace conference of 1919. The Allied leaders, from left to right, Lloyd George, Orlando, Clemenceau (known as 'The Tiger') and Woodrow Wilson, depart while a child, who will be an adult by 1940, sheds tears over the peace treaty whose harsh terms would help lead to World War II. It is an extraordinarily prophetic drawing.

Above and below: Fascism and its variants were rife in many countries in the 1930s, as these two cartoons illustrate. Among those trying to net the National Socialist bacillus in the French cartoon 'Vain efforts' are Uncle Sam, Marianne and John Bull. The powerful drawing of Mussolini as the mother wolf from Rome's Capitoline Hill is by the Egyptian artist Kimon Marengo (1904-88), better known as 'Kem.' In place of Romulus and Remus are infant fascists Hitler, Kemal Attaturk, Metaxas of Greece and Franco, with Britain's Oswald Mosley waiting his turn. The ancient Roman symbol of power, the *fasces* – comprising rods for beating and an axe for execution – was adopted by Mussolini, giving rise to the name 'Fascist.'

Dictators all
Kem, Christmas card, December 1936

THE GIRLS HE LEFT BEHIND HIM.

David Low, *Evening Standard*, 10 May 1935

The Italian answer to British arms control
Il 420, n.d.

Top: Mussolini's invasion of Abyssinia (now Ethiopia) in October 1935 was much caricatured at the time. The New Zealand-born cartoonist David Low (1891-1963) shows Hitler and his henchmen Hermann Goering and Joseph Goebbels happily waving Mussolini off on his conquest of Africa while they get on with plundering Europe. (This cartoon caused Low's drawings to be banned in Italy.) Italy's answer to British sanctions and demands for arms limitations at this time is clearly stated in the illustration from *Il 420 (above)*.

It would not be true to say that the rise of Hitler and the Nazis was completely unopposed in Germany itself, though 17 million voted for him as Chancellor in 1933. Many cartoonists working for the Munich-based satirical weekly *Simplicissimus* (1896-1944) took a strong stand against the Nazi movement, Karl Arnold (1883-1953) foremost among them. Remarkably, the magazine continued well into the war (it was eventually closed down in 1944), though by 1939 many of the contributors had fled overseas and those who remained had adapted their styles, willingly or otherwise, to attacks on the Allies. 'Master-Race,' like 'Der Münchner' (*overleaf*), pokes fun at early members of the Nazi Party and their obsession with the ancient swastika motif (from the Sanskrit word for good luck). Remember, too, that this was drawn nine years before Hitler became Chancellor.

Master-Race
Karl Arnold, *Simplicissimus*, 1924

The bloody-handed thug in the drawing by Paul Iribe (1883-1935), 'We speak French,' has a more sinister tone – Hitler's book, *Mein Kampf*, which among other things promised the destruction of France, was currently a bestseller in Germany. (Note it is a French edition in his hand.)

'Barlons Vranzais'
Paul Iribe, 1933

13

**'Those who may try to attack will come up against shattering resistance.
Let them not put their pig's snout into the Soviet kitchen garden' (Stalin)**

Kukryniksi, Soviet poster, 1935

Above: The Soviet poster by the Kukryniksi group has no illusions about the Nazi threat. The pseudonym 'Kukryniksi' derives from the combined names of the three artists who made up the group: Mikhail Kupryanov (1903-91), Porfiry Krylov (1902-90) and Nikolay Sokolov (b. 1903).

Der Münchner

Mei' Ruah mocht' i hamm und a Revolution.
A Ordnung muaß sei' und a Judenpogrom.
A Diktator g'hört hera und glei' duvu'u'huut
Mir zoagen's Enk scho', wia ma Deutschland aufbaut'

Karl Arnold, *Simplicissimus*, 3 December 1923

Hitler's early supporters came from the Munich beer halls, as Arnold's cartoon suggests. The caption to 'Munich Man' reads: 'What I want is a bit of peace and a revolution, law and order and a pogrom for the Jews. We should get hold of a dictator and then get rid of him. We'll show you how to build up Germany.'
Opposite: Hitler greatly admired Frederick the Great. The 1932 caricature, 'Hail Prussia!', shows Frederick behind Hitler, with a parody of one of the Prussian king's most famous sayings. The cartoon version reads: 'In my state every man can only be happy my way!' (Frederick's original said: 'In my state every man can be happy in his own way.')

SIMPLICISSIMUS

Herausgabe: München   BEGRÜNDET VON ALBERT LANGEN UND TH. TH. HEINE   Postversand: Stuttgart

Heil Preußen!

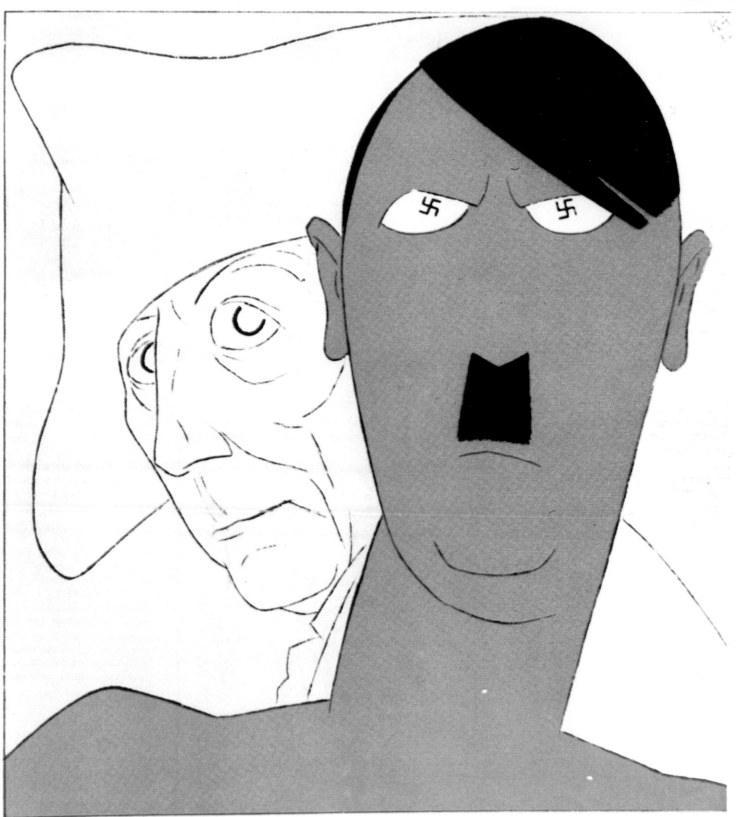

„In Meinem Staate kann jeder nur nach Meiner Façon selig werden!"

Karl Arnold, *Simplicissimus*, 15 May 1932

15

'Take me to Czechoslovakia, driver'
Vaughn Shoemaker, *Chicago Daily News*, 1938

What next?
Daniel Fitzpatrick, *St Louis Post-Dispatch*, 25 September 1938

The annexation by Germany of the predominantly German-speaking part of Czechoslovakia known as the Sudetenland caused international concern; many correctly saw this as a prelude to further demands which indeed resulted in the eventual destruction of the Czech state. The taxi-driver cartoon by Vaughn Shoemaker (1902-91) and the powerful Nazi steamroller by Daniel Fitzpatrick (1891-1969), with Czechoslovakia crushed beneath, both won international acclaim.

'Would you oblige me with a match, please?'
David Low, *Evening Standard*, 25 February 1938

War or peace? By the late 1930s the answer seemed inevitable. Low shows British Prime Minister Neville Chamberlain holding a picture of anti-appeaser Anthony Eden, who had just resigned as Foreign Secretary in protest at the continued vacillation of the government. The figure requesting a light is Low's composite dictator 'Muzzler,' introduced when measures were taken to tone down the artist's personal attacks on Hitler and Mussolini. The *Evening Standard* and all newspapers printing Low's cartoons had been officially banned from Germany after his drawing 'It worked at the Reichstag – why not here?' (18 November 1933) – showing Hitler setting fire to the League of Nations building – and from Italy after 'The girls he left behind him' (see p. 12). In Shoemaker's team of American football giants bearing down on the diminutive peaceful nations (*right*), Japan has been included following her invasion of China in July 1937. Mars, the god of war, carries the world as their football behind.

16

**'Come on in, I'll treat you right.
I used to know your daddy'**
Clarence D Batchelor, *New York Daily News*, 1936

The Spanish Civil War (1936-9) was a proving ground for the Nazis and the Fascists, who supported General Franco's right-wing revolt against the democratically elected Popular Front government of Manuel Azaña. Clarence Batchelor's universal theme (*above*) won him great acclaim in the USA and elsewhere, and a Pulitzer Prize in 1937. (Note the scrolled borders, a common feature of Batchelor's work.) Born in Kansas in 1888, Batchelor died in Connecticut in 1978.

1938's Four Horsemen
Vaughn Shoemaker, *Chicago Daily News*, 1938

Ritualmord-Saison bei Streicher
Ritual Murder Season at Streicher's
Saison de crimes rituels chez M. Streicher

„Keine Zeit jetzt! Wir feiern doch gerade Pessach..."

„We have no time just now. We are celebrating the Passover..."

„Pas l'temps, à présent! Vous savez bien que nous sommes en train de fêter le „Pessach!"

Bert, *Juden Christen Heiden im III Reich*, Prague, 1935

Der Stürmer (cover), March 1940

Hitler's account of his struggle for power, *Mein Kampf*, outlined his vision of a new European order to be run by a *Herrenvolk* or 'master race' of pure Aryan peoples under the direction of the archetypically Aryan Germans. The vitriolic cartoon by the Czech artist Bert (*opposite*) depicts Julius Streicher, the editor of the violently anti-Semitic weekly newspaper, *Der Stürmer*, at his desk. Streicher was later executed by the Allies as a war criminal. Note the 'pure Aryan' illustrated second from top right, the comparison between flat Semitic and domed Aryan skulls and the ritual murder statistics chart for 1935 pinned up in the adjacent laboratory. *Above* is a typical front cover from *Der Stürmer* with a drawing by the resident cartoonist, Fips. The strapline at the bottom, which reads, 'The Jews are our misfortune,' ran in every issue.

The German New Heathen
Bert, *Juden Christen Heiden im III Reich*, Prague, 1935

Those who were not privileged to be members of the Nazi *Herrenvolk* were classed as *Untermensch* (subhumans) and as such had to be eliminated like a disease. Prominent among these were Jews, Slavs, Communists and Blacks. The powerful drawings by the Czech artist Bert come from a collection entitled *Jews, Christians and Heathens in the Third Reich* published in German, French and English. The Nordic German monster is seen devouring a clergyman and a rabbi on the cover and – with the image of Hitler in the background – tramples sundry churchmen underfoot in the name of Aryan supremacy in the illustration captioned 'The German New Heathen'. (The cartoon is subtitled, 'Our Aryan myth is: "Love your neighbor – by tearing him to pieces!"') Joseph Flatter (1894-1988), an ex-patriate Austrian said to have been the cartoonist most feared by Hitler, gloriously lampoons the fat German burgher and his family as members of the *Herrenvolk* in one of a series of illustrations made to accompany quotations from *Mein Kampf*.

Opposite: Ralph Soupault's full-page cartoon from the French satirical weekly *Gringoire* wonders what Hitler's madness is: megalomania, kleptomania, paranoia etc, or simply Nazism, a mixture of all the basest instincts?

The Herrenvolk's dream
Joseph Flatter, *Mein Kampf*, 1939

Bert, *Juden Christen Heiden im III Reich* (cover), Prague, 1935

Mais quelle est sa folie ?

PAR RALPH SOUPAULT

EST-CE LA MYTHOMANIE ?
– Tendance pathologique à échafauder des mensonges et des fables...

LA MONOMANIE ?
Essentiellement caractérisée par le délire de la persécution...

LA KLEPTOMANIE ?
ou manie du vol...

LA DIPSOMANIE ?
Tendance maladive à boire sans cesse...

LA MÉGALOMANIE ?
ou délire des grandeurs...

LA NÉCROPHILIE ?
Perversion qui cherche sa satisfaction sur des cadavres...

LA PARANOÏA
ou dégénérescence : Les criminels sont souvent des dégénérés.

ou, tout simplement LE NAZISME ?
Mélange de tous les délires, aberrations, vésanies et instincts criminels...

Ralph Soupault, *Gringoire*, 14 September 1939

EINZELPREIS **30** PF.
Schweiz 50 Rappen, Italien Lire 1,25
Ausland mit ermäßigtem Porto 27 Pfg.
übriges Ausland 32 Pfg.
Danzig 40 Guldenpfennig

8. JAHRGANG / FOLGE 18 / 3. MAI 1938

DIE BRENNESSEL

VERLAG FRANZ EHER NACHF. GMBH. BERLIN SW 68

„Väterchen" in feinem Jagdzimmer

Träumerei an einem Moskauer Kamin

Seppla, *Die Brennessel* (cover), 3 May 1938

The front cover by Seppla (Josef Plank) for the Berlin satirical magazine *Die Brennessel*, entitled '"Little Father" in his den: dream in a Moscow hunting-lodge,' has Stalin dozing beside a hearth filled with the bones of his enemies, their heads mounted above. The cover appeared shortly after the purges in which Stalin had the majority of the Red Army's leading generals killed.

'The only way we can save her'
Carey Orr, *Chicago Tribune*, 1939

Above: An example of the strong non-interventionist lobby in the United States that prevailed until the Japanese attack on Pearl Harbor in December 1941. Carey Orr (1890-1967) was a powerful voice for conservatism and patriotism; he was to be awarded a Pulitzer prize in 1961. The opposite view is taken in the *Daily Herald* cartoon by Will Dyson (*left*), drawn in the month of his death and printed posthumously. Here the rearmament movement is depicted as a fat Mae West realist in contrast to the tattered and forlorn figure of peace standing on a pedestal and out of touch with the world, her arms filled with insincere pledges of friendship.

Will Dyson, *Daily Herald*, January 1939

23

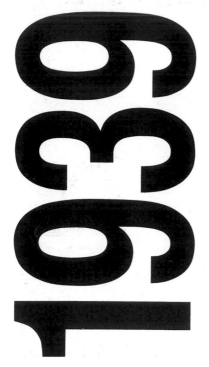

1939

After Hitler's forces marched into Prague in March 1939, Chamberlain dropped his policy of appeasement and drew up mutual assistance treaties with Poland, Rumania and Greece, effectively committing Britain and France to war if one of these countries was attacked by Germany. With the Italo-German 'Pact of Steel' in May, which formalized the earlier 'Axis' accord, sabres began to be rattled. When erstwhile opponents Nazi Germany and the Soviet Union signed a Non-Aggression Pact in August, the probable became the inevitable. Germany attacked Poland on 1 September. Britain, France, Australia and New Zealand declared war on Germany two days later, with South Africa and Canada following suit shortly after. Faced by vastly superior German forces, and also invaded by the Soviet Union from the east, Poland fell within the month. Despite their declaration of war, Britain and France effectively did little to help, remaining shaken but temporarily safe behind their boundaries.

The general expectation was that the outbreak of war would swiftly lead to protracted trench warfare in Europe and large-scale strategic bombing of civilians. Thousands of children were evacuated from cities and huge defenseworks – which had been built along national boundaries in the 1920s and 1930s – were rapidly manned. However, for the rest of 1939 the only major fighting in Europe came when the Soviet Union invaded Finland in November. But this period of 'Phony War' was to prove only a lull before the storm.

WONDER HOW LONG THE HONEYMOON WILL LAST?

Clifford Berryman, *Washington Star*, 9 October 1939

Rendezvous
David Low, *Evening Standard*, 20 September 1939

The Nazi-Soviet Pact of Non-Aggression signed on 23 August 1939 shook the Allies, who had been negotiating with the Soviet Union themselves. The Pulitzer prize-winning cartoonist of the *Washington Star*, Clifford Berryman (1869-1949), has Hitler and Stalin getting married (*left*), with Stalin as an apparently satisfied bride. Henri Gassier (1883-1951), in the Parisian journal *La Lumière*, points out the difficulties of reconciling the Nazi-Soviet Pact with Hitler's own words reviling Communism in *Mein Kampf*. (Note the pun on the titles of Hitler's biography and of Karl Marx's *Das Kapital*.)

Above: The German Army invaded Poland at 0445 hours on 1 September 1939. Unable to resist the German *Blitzkrieg* (lightning war), the Poles were also faced with a separate invasion by the Soviet Union on 17 September. The occupation of Poland was soon complete and Hitler and Stalin divided the country between them. In David Low's famous cartoon, the two unlikely allies congratulate each other over the body of Poland.

War camouflage
H P Gassier, *La Lumière*, 1939

25

The Two Constrictors

'I don't know about helping you, Adolf, but I *do* understand your point of view'
Bernard Partridge, *Punch*, 8 November 1939

After the defeat of Poland a strange unease settled over Europe. The initial *blitzkrieg* was succeeded by the *Sitzkrieg* – 'sitting war' – when the Germans and the Allies were apparently content to glare at each other from behind their great defensive fortifications, the Maginot Line and the Westwall (or Siegfried Line). The great momentum of Nazi conquest appeared to have ground to a halt, as Thomas's exhausted Hitler snail (*below*) illustrates. The Welsh cartoonist, Bert Thomas (1883-1966) was perhaps best known for his famous World War I drawing 'Arf a mo', Kaiser,' but he also did considerable work in World War II, including an equally memorable poster, 'Is your journey really necessary?' (see p. 97).

A popular song during this period – also known as the Twilight or Phony War – was 'We're Gonna Hang Out the Washing on the Siegfried Line' and cartoonists were quick to seize the opportunity to caricature this sense of false optimism. A delightful example is the drawing (*right*) by 'Pont', whose real name was Graham Laidler (1908-40). This picture of life in the British Expeditionary Force – Britain's small army in Europe commanded by Lord Gort – is from his 'Popular Misconceptions' series in *Punch*. The German cartoonists reacted swiftly and the *Das Reich* drawing has a caption which reads: "'What's the Englander doing here?' "He begged me to let him hang out his washing on the Siegfried Line just one more time, sergeant."' (Note the nesting storks as a sign of military inactivity.)

Above: Another view of the destruction of Poland. Bernard Partridge has the two dictators as boa constrictors with Poland their latest territorial acquisition. (Notice that Stalin, with teeth, is by far the larger and more dominant of the two snakes.)

Bert Thomas, *Evening News*, 1 November 1939

Popular Misconceptions – Life in the BEF
Pont, *Punch*, 13 December 1939

Westwallidyll

'Was macht denn der Engländer hier?'

'Herr Unteroffizier, er hat so sehr gebeten, nur ein einziges Mal seine Wäsche an der
Siegfriedlinie aufhängen zu dürfen!'
Das Reich, 1939

Boomerangski!

H B Armstrong, *Melbourne Argus*, 11 December 1939

Left: Stalin's invasion of neighboring Finland failed to emulate Hitler's *Blitzkrieg* on Poland. Though the initial attack on 30 November 1939 had considerable success, the Finns quickly rallied behind their Mannerheim Line defenses and kept up fierce resistance, in the face of an army many times larger than their own, until 12 March the following year. The difficulty the mighty Soviets had in conquering such a small nation suggested to Hitler and the Allies alike (with some satisfaction on both sides) that the Russians, following Stalin's purges of the Red Army's officer corps, lacked the training and technology for modern warfare.

Below left: A cutting anti-American cartoon entitled 'Blood and Business' by the Soviet artist Boris Efimov (b. 1900), drawn at a time when the Nazi-Soviet Pact was still very much in force. Using a skull abacus, Uncle Sam keeps a tally of his war profits as the news from Europe is announced on the radio.

Below: This joke by the French cartoonist Maurice Henry shows a rural scene with two French soldiers whispering as an annoyed *curé* tramps past: 'He is furious . . . there is bromide in his communion wine!' (Sodium and potassium bromides were introduced into beverages consumed by troops to dampen their sexual appetites.)

La drôle de guerre

**'Il est furieux . . .
Y a du bromure dans son vin de messe!'**

Maurice Henry, *Le canard enchaîné*, 22 November 1939

Boris Efimov, 1940

The Sower
Sidney Strube, *Daily Express*, 1939

' "Nobby," my old missus said, "if there was only two mines in
all the blinking hatlantic you'd 'it 'em!" '
Ian Fenwick, *Enter Trubshaw*, London, 1944

Though the Allies were relatively
inactive in Europe during the
Phony War, the war at sea
proceeded apace. The Royal Navy
blockaded German supply-lines and
harassed the battleship *Admiral
Graf Spee* – leading to her eventual
scuttling outside Montevideo
harbour on 17 December after the
Battle of the River Plate. On the
negative side, however, was the
Germans' potent naval weapon: the
magnetic mine. This was to prove
disastrous to both Allied and
neutral shipping – 79 ships being
sunk in 1939 alone – until
'degaussing' (circulating an electric
current around a ship's hull to
neutralize the magnetic field) was
introduced. In the drawing by
Sidney Strube (1891-1956), one of
the most popular British
cartoonists of the period, mines
appear as the seeds of death.
Special Air Service (SAS) major
Ian Fenwick was a schoolboy
colleague of actor David Niven and
a regular contributor to journals
such as *London Opinion* before his
death in action in 1944.

England's Selbsteinkreisung

Karl Arnold, *Simplicissimus*, 15 October 1939

As well as the new magnetic mines, German U-boats took a considerable toll of Allied and neutral shipping, especially in the Atlantic, until the introduction of the convoy system. Indeed, such was the success of the 'wolf packs' that between July and October 1940 217 merchant ships were sunk in what came to be known to the U-boat commanders as 'Die glückliche Zeit' (the happy time). Karl Arnold shows an aged John Bull cowering beneath Chamberlain's umbrella from the light of a death's-head moon and surrounded by U-boats. The title reads: 'England's self-encirclement: danger from above and below, a situation difficult to escape from.' Fips' drawing for *Der Stürmer* has John Bull's legs perforated with torpedoes, with the caption: 'Damn, that's the limit. How much longer will I be able to stand?' The Allied response has First Lord of the Admiralty Winston Churchill, renowned for his liking for cigars, smoking two U-boats at a time in Armstrong's cartoon. Strube's John Bull, in the guise of Popeye the Sailor, puffs convoy pipe-smoke over an irate Donald Duck in German naval uniform.

Sidney Strube, *Daily Express*, 14 September 1939

Cigar-in-the-face Win

H B Armstrong, *Melbourne Argus*, January 1940

Der torpedierte John Bull

Fips, *Der Stürmer*, No 43, October 1939

München, 25. Februar 1940
45. Jahrgang / Nummer 8

30 Pfennig

SiMPLiCiSSiMUS

VERLAG KNORR & HIRTH KOMMANDITGESELLSCHAFT, MÜNCHEN

Der Konflikt

(R. Kriesch)

„Als Mensch möchte ich nichts sagen, aber als Luftschutzwart kann ich das absolut nicht dulden!"

R Kriesch, *Simplicissimus*, 25 February 1940

Blackout regulations to ensure that cities could not be seen from the air, and hence would be less likely to be targets for enemy bombers, caused considerable confusion and many accidents in the streets on both sides during the war. The joke by Walter is typical of the genre. Germany also produced blackout jokes as the *Simplicissimus* cartoon 'The Conflict' shows. The caption reads: 'As a man I would like to say nothing, but as an air-raid warden I cannot possibly do so.'

'Well, it was your idea to have a black cat!'
John G Walter, *Punch*, 15 November 1939

'I knew I'd hung the darn thing somewhere'
Timothy Hailstone, *Punch*, 6 May 1940

'What do you mean – "Look up there?" – I can't see anything out of the ordinary'
Fougasse, *Sorry – No Rubber*, London, 1942

Non-dirigible barrage balloons were used by both sides as a precaution against low-flying aircraft attack and were particularly effective at night. Kenneth Bird (1887-1965), later to become editor of *Punch*, drew under the name of 'Fougasse' (from the French for a kind of anti-personnel mine) and is perhaps best known for his 'Careless Talk Costs Lives' posters (see page 142). The Hailstone gag is typical of the vast number produced on the topic of barrage balloons.

Three popular wartime magazines. *Lustige Blätter* was published weekly by Erich Zander Verlag in Berlin and was already in its fifty-eighth year by the time of the issue shown, 31 December 1942. (The captions reads: 'The world turns on its axis.') *Lilliput* (*below left*) was founded in 1937 and featured over eighty covers (all with the distinctive black dog) by the Czech artist Walter Trier (1890-1951), who had been a regular contributor to *Lustige Blätter* before emigrating to England. The issue shown is for January 1941 (note the Anderson shelter). Arthur Szyk's stunning covers for the American weekly, *Collier's*, are well represented elsewhere in this book. The example below is by the London-born illustrator Lawson Wood (1878-1957).

Lustige Blätter (cover), 31 December 1942

Lilliput (cover), January 1941

Collier's (cover) 8 May 1943

تقدمُ التعَاونِ الألمَانى الروسيّ

The progress of Russian and German cooperation
Kem, Middle East poster, 1939

Another view of the Nazi-Soviet
Pact. Kem's delightful poster for
the Middle East has Stalin and
Hitler embarking on a three-legged
race with only one serviceable boot
between them.

The gun that jammed
Bert Thomas, *Evening News*, November 1939

Bert Thomas, *Evening News*, 8 September 1939

Buriko, *Il 420*, 1939

'There are only the three regulars left now, sir'
Anton, *Punch*, 8 November 1939

Opposite: The propaganda war on both sides in the early days of the conflict mostly centered around radio broadcasts or the dropping of aerial leaflets. In these two Bert Thomas cartoons, von Ribbentrop, German Foreign Minister, and Goebbels, the German Minister for Propaganda, are seen being halted or trapped by the truth emanating from Britain.

Above: This cartoon compares Italy in 1919 and 1939. The 1919 Italy is seen as a weak *fasces* armed only with a club, contemplating the ruins of the Roman Empire. The same country in 1939 appears as a muscular figure, now brandishing a rifle and pistol, who strides forward to conquer Djibouti (French Somaliland) via Tunis and Suez.

Left: 'Anton' was originally (1937) the pseudonym of Antonia Yeoman and her brother Harold Thompson. However, as time progressed, Antonia increasingly took on complete cartoons and later continued under the *nom de plume* on her own until her death in June 1970. This cartoon comments both on the eagerness of governments for new ideas in the weapons field and the difficulty of taking a balanced view of the suggestions submitted.

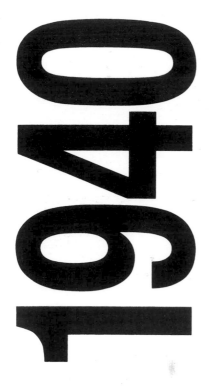

In April 1940 the Phony War came abruptly to an end with the German invasion of Denmark and Norway. The following month, Germany struck against the Netherlands, Belgium and France. The techniques of *Blitzkrieg* made static fortifications, such as the Maginot Line, totally worthless. A new kind of warfare had arrived and the Allies had nothing to counter it. By the end of June France was defeated and Hitler was free to impose his New Order on mainland Europe.

However, by what seemed a miracle, about 200,000 British and 140,000 French troops had escaped to Britain from Dunkirk at the beginning of June. Under the leadership of a new prime minister, Winston Churchill, Britain stood in solitary defiance of Nazi power. On 13 August Goering's Luftwaffe began an all-out air offensive in Britain. At the same time, over 2000 troop transports were amassed at the French Channel ports in preparation for Operation Sealion – seaborne assaults on Folkestone, Eastbourne and Brighton. But the invasion never came. It was postponed repeatedly as the Luftwaffe fought for air supremacy against the RAF, and eventually cancelled.

After the Battle of Britain the Allies had some cause for hope – despite the fearful bombardment known as the Blitz – and victories over the Italians, who had joined the war in June, produced small rays of sunshine in an otherwise gloomy outlook. Inspired by Churchill's forceful oratory, Britain and what remained of the original Allies could begin to draw breath.

De Robot

L J Jordaan, *De Groene Amsterdammer*, 1940

The unstoppable war machine. This fine graphic illustration of the Nazi robot by L J Jordaan is all the more remarkable in that it was published in the underground newspaper *De Groene Amsterdammer* in occupied Holland.

David Low's immortal character, Colonel Blimp, featured every week in his *Evening Standard* full-page 'Topical Budget' composite cartoon from 21 April 1934 until paper shortages in 1940 stopped the page altogether. (However the character continued to appear in cartoons thereafter.) At a time when the dictators were calling themselves the *true* democrats and advocating *real* freedom, that had every appearance of slavery, Low needed a symbol typifying the disposition to 'mixed-up thinking, to having it both ways, to dogmatic doubleness, to paradox and plain self-contradiction.' He hit upon the name when overhearing a conversation in a Turkish bath about a colonel who, protesting about the mechanization of the cavalry, had insisted that, even if the horses went, the uniforms etc should stay and the troops must wear spurs in their tanks. From then on the Colonel appeared regularly in the column – usually clad only in a bath towel and in conversation with a cartoon Low – uttering such absurdities as 'Hitler only needs arms so that he can declare peace on the rest of the world,' 'The League of Nations is a big sham. Why, it's nearly all foreigners' and 'Look at those foreign agitators sapping the Constitution! We need a dictator like Mussolini.'

By 1938 the Colonel's sayings had been translated into 24 languages and the word 'blimp' had passed into the dictionaries, albeit in a mistaken definition. For Low, 'He does NOT represent a coherent reactionary outlook so much as slapdash stupidity.' However, Low's creation began to take on a life of its own. A film, *The Life and Death of Colonel Blimp* (1943) was banned for depicting the British Army as fools, the Soviet cartoonist Efimov used the character to lampoon British delays in forming a Second Front, and Low himself invented 'Blimpski' to counter *Pravda*'s attacks. The version shown here is from a collection of humorous press ephemera reprinted from the *New Statesman and Nation*'s 'This England' column.

David Low, *This England* (cover), London, 1940

After the Nazi/Soviet destruction of Poland and the eventual defeat of Finland by the Soviet Union, the natural thought of the world's governments was 'Where next?' Leslie Illingworth (1902-79) was born in Wales. In 1939 he took over Poy's position on the *Daily Mail* while still continuing to contribute to *Punch*. His cartoons here are remarkably prophetic as to the course of the war in the next few months – note the German paratroop monster crawling towards a port with evident Dutch-gable buildings (*right*) and the fact that only the Rumanian fish faces the Stalin cat while the others look toward Hitler (*below left*). In Sidney Strube's music-hall act (*left*) the four revolvers form a swastika while Adolf stands near a ceremonial sword representing broken pledges. All the guns are cocked to fire but of the onlookers only Belgium wears a steel helmet in expectation of war.

Four-gun Adolf, the Blitzkrieg Kid, now appearing at the Neutrality Theatre
Sidney Strube, *Daily Express*, 22 January 1940

'What me? I never touch goldfish!'
Leslie Illingworth, *Daily Mail*, 17 November 1939

The Combat
Leslie Illingworth, *Punch*, 6 November 1939

NORWAY
IRON ORE
FOR EXPORT

THE IRON COMES BACK

David Low, *Evening Standard*, 25 April 1940

**'We shall remain strictly neutral
and defend our
territorial integrity at all costs'**
Osbert Lancaster,
Daily Express, 16 April 1940

On 9 April 1940 Hitler invaded Denmark and Norway. Copenhagen fell in 12 hours and the Norwegian government and royal family left Oslo the following day, the pro-Nazi Vidkun Quisling being placed in charge of a puppet government. Norwegian forces, aided by British and French troops together with the Royal Navy, resisted fiercely, but Allied disorganization in the face of a well-disciplined foe ultimately led to defeat by 9 June.

Osbert Lancaster (1908-86) was the inventor and acknowledged master of the one-frame 'pocket' cartoon. In this example from the *Daily Express*, for whom he worked from 1 January 1939 until his death, he satirizes the stance of countries such as Poland and Denmark, already overcome by aggressors. He seems also to suggest that the only safe place left is the South Pole (there are no penguins in the Arctic). Low's drawing comments on the fact that the Norwegians had ironically contributed to their own downfall by supplying mineral ores to Germany for arms production in the 1930s.

lünchen, 14. Juli 1940
5. Jahrgang / Nummer 28

30 Pfennig

SiMPLiCiSSiMUS

VERLAG KNORR & HIRTH KOMMANDITGESELLSCHAFT, MÜNCHEN

Jeanne d'Arc

(Karl Arnold)

„Hoffentlich floß Frankreichs Blut zum letzten Mal für England!"
"É a sperare che la Francia abbia sparso per l' ultima volta il suo sangue per l' Inghilterra !"

Karl Arnold, *Simplicissimus*, 14 July 1940

With the threat to the British Empire from the Nazi occupation of the mainland of Europe, the United States was becoming increasingly concerned about the future of world democracy and especially about whether she should get involved in another war. The 'last bulwark against totalitarianism' image finds expression in this poster (*below*) of the Churchillian bulldog holding the line.

Henri Guignon, US poster, 1940

The Germans entered Paris on 13 June 1940 and by the 21st the French had signed an armistice. To add to France's humiliation Hitler deliberately chose the site of the signing – the Forest of Compiègne, Oise – and the very railway carriage (specially moved from its museum) in which the Germans had surrendered in 1918. The terms of the armistice were heavy: north and west France were to be occupied by the Germans. The rest was to be administered by Great War veteran Marshal Pétain and his pro-Nazi deputy Laval from a new capital at the spa town of Vichy, near Lyons. The victorious Germans constantly harped on the theme of the British betrayal of the French – Karl Arnold's moving picture of Joan of Arc floating over Notre-Dame cathedral and the ruins of Paris has great effect. The caption, which since 28 April 1941 *Simplicissimus* printed in Italian as well for distribution of the paper to Germany's new wartime allies, reads: 'Hopefully, France's blood flows for the last time for England.'

German propaganda postcard, c1940

Schach dem King!

German propaganda postcard, c1940

With Britain alone and on the defensive, the Axis nations took every opportunity to lampoon the once-mighty empire. In the first postcard cartoon (*top*), John Bull is seen stealing Norwegian merchant ships, gold reserves and antiquities from the Low Countries, and battleships from France. 'Check to the King' has George VI in the last corner of the board hemmed in by paratroops, U-boats, Stuka dive-bombers and a panzer tank. Churchill can be seen hurrying to join the Royal Navy and merchant marine ships already removed from the board, while Chamberlain lies flat out and three Jewish plutocrats shed buckets of tears.

A totalitarian eclipse has been arranged
Philip Zec, *Daily Mirror*, 1940

Following the Allied failure in Norway, unrest amongst the British people and Parliament about the conduct of the war led to the resignation of Chamberlain and the formation of a coalition government under Churchill. The powerful 'eclipse' image by Philip Zec (1910-83) shows public approval of the new government leader. An interesting contrast is between Low's famous 'All behind you, Winston' drawing and Bogner's 'England awake!' In the German cartoon we see Churchill as a flabby businessman too small for his boots, wearing a Star of David armband and armed only with an umbrella. The mangy British Lion is now too skinny for its collar. The caption reads: 'This is the man who claims to free the German people from the "barbarity of the authoritarian regimes."'

Der Mann, der auszog, um das deutsche Volk von der 'Barbarei des autoritären Regimes' zu befreien
Bogner, *Das Schwarze Korps*, 6 June 1940

'All behind you, Winston'
David Low, *Evening Standard*, 14 May 1940

The angels of peace descend on Belgium
David Low, *Evening Standard*, 10 June 1940

With the German invasion of the Low Countries on 10 May 1940, the Phony War came to an abrupt end. Violating the neutrality of Belgium and Holland, the Nazi forces flashed across the lowlands, leaving the French Maginot Line, which stopped short at the Belgian frontier, totally exposed on its flank. The Dutch government and royal family fled to London on 13 May and after heavy aerial bombardment of the port of Rotterdam the following day, Holland capitulated. The conquest completed, Hitler appointed the Austrian Artur von Seyss-Inquart as governor of Holland, and he immediately began a reign of terror over its inhabitants.

The cartoon for the Free Dutch newspaper, *Vrij Nederland*, published in London and air-dropped into Holland by the RAF, has the caption: 'Resist my system, then you will see my real face!' Seyss-Inquart holds a poster

Sabotage in Nederland
Vicky, *Vrij Nederland*, 24 August 1940

declaring 'Death Penalty on Grand Scale for Sabotage,' while over a picture of a worried-looking Hitler has been daubed 'Get Rid of Hitler – Free Holland.' Vicky, whose real name was Victor Weisz (1913-66), was a Hungarian Jew born in Berlin. He was a regular contributor to the radical anti-Hitler paper *12 Uhr Blatt* until its acquisition by the Nazis forced him to flee first to Hungary and then to London.

Above: After the fall of Holland, Belgian resistance soon collapsed. On 28 May King Leopold agreed to surrender – a decision much disputed later. As with all Germany's conquests, once Belgium had been occupied, the sinister secret police, the Gestapo, moved in – under the direction of its head, Heinrich Himmler – to deal with 'subversive elements' in the name of restoring peace. Low's Belgian cartoon has great power.

The Luftwaffe's 'Blitz' on London began on 7 September 1940 and bombing soon extended to include all the major ports and industrial areas of Britain – Coventry being particularly badly hit. The destruction was enormous. The German poster for Belgium (*right*) has Churchill broadcasting words of confidence while all around him the world collapses in ruins ('Madame la Marquise' was a popular song of the time). The coincidental use (*below*) of the Imperial Roman thumb symbol – deriving from the days of Colosseum gladiator entertainments – by the Italian Gino Boccasile (1900-52) and the American Daniel Fitzpatrick is quite remarkable, though it is interesting to note that Fitzpatrick uses St Paul's rather than Tower Bridge as the main building shown.

Right: A superb characterization by Arthur Szyk (1894-1951) of how Hitler and the Axis powers viewed the New World Order. As well as Hitler seated on the *Untermensch* rug – while Uncle Sam and John Bull plead in chains – appear (from right) a Japanese soldier, a German field marshal, Mussolini (with fan), Goering, Himmler, Laval (with a puppet Pétain) and Goebbels. (The wording on Hitler's throne reads: 'I am the Holy Ghost.') Szyk, who was born in Poland, fought in the Imperial Russian Army in World War I and worked as a cartoonist in England in 1939 before emigrating to the United States the following year.

The spirit of London
Daniel Fitzpatrick, *St Louis Post-Dispatch*, 1940

Gino Boccasile, Italian poster, 1940

A Madman's Dream
Arthur Szyk, *The New Order*, New York, 1940

'Very well, alone'
David Low, *Evening Standard*, 18 June 1940

With the fall of France, Britain was indeed fighting alone against Germany and Italy. The image of dogged resilience the British like to project in times of adversity was well typified in Churchill's famous speech, 'We shall fight on the beaches . . . We shall never surrender,' broadcast on 4 June, and in perhaps the best remembered Allied drawing of the whole war – Low's 'Very well, alone,' a tremendously evocative image.

'So our poor empire is alone in the world.'
'Aye, we are – the whole five hundred million of us.'
Fougasse, *Punch*, 17 July 1940

'Go to it'
Sidney Strube, *Daily Express*, 8 June 1940

Another powerful picture of British grit is that conjured up by Strube's bulldog Churchill with a tin hat bearing a slogan familiar from British Ministry of Information posters: 'Go to it!' (later versions added: 'and keep at it'). What is so easy to forget, of course, is that there was considerably more to the British Empire at this time than just the United Kingdom, as Fougasse's drawing so wittily comments (*top*).

Tim, Paris, 1940

The triumphant English retreat
Buriko, *Il 420*, 1940

After the occupation of the Low Countries and the drive through the Ardennes forest, the German forces made short work of Allied resistance in northern France and by 26 May the British Expeditionary Force and what was left of the other Allied armies in the northern sector were bottled up in the port of Dunkirk between Calais and the Belgian border. Miraculously, instead of the 30,000 troops they expected to save, the Royal Navy, aided by a vast flotilla of small craft from Britain, managed to rescue more than ten times that number of Allied troops. The French Army fought on after Dunkirk but the power of the German advance proved too great, and armistice negotiations began in June.

Among the evacuees from the Continent was the future leader of the Free French government, General Charles de Gaulle – seen being carried ashore by Churchill in the cartoon (*left*) by the Polish-born artist Louis Mitelberg ('Tim,' b. 1919). In reality, De Gaulle flew in from France on 17 June.

Not unnaturally, the Axis interpretation of events was somewhat different, as the Italian cartoon above bears witness. The image of an army fighting a brilliant rearguard action is nowhere to be seen in Buriko's drawing of galloping retreat.

Below: Italy declared war on the Allies on 10 June 1940 after considerable courting by both sides. In Shepard's drawing Goebbels is about to pull an anxious-looking Mussolini into the wasteland of Germany where his future is uncertain. By contrast the Allied side of the wall has a soft landing assured and the garden is blooming. Ernest H Shepard (1879-1972) is perhaps best remembered today for his illustrations to *Winnie-the-Pooh* and *The Wind in the Willows*, but he was also a regular contributor to *Punch* from 1902.

Humpty Dumpty and the Roman Wall
E H Shepard, *Punch*, 8 May 1940

The Dream and the Nightmare
David Low, *Evening Standard*, 2 May 1940

David Low, *Evening Standard*, 11 June 1940

Two more comments on the changing face of Europe at this time. Low's famous cartoon of 'The Harmony Boys' has Hitler conducting Mussolini, Stalin and a diminutive Franco (representing pro-Nazi Spain), while 'The Dream and the Nightmare' depicts the possibility of disaster from an Italian alliance with Germany (note the peace plan from President Roosevelt on the table).

'. . . meanwhile, in Britain, the entire population, faced by the threat of invasion, has been flung into a state of complete panic . . .'
Pont, *Punch*, 14 August 1940

'Ignore it, Carruthers, it's just another move in the war of nerves'
Osbert Lancaster, *New Pocket Cartoons*, London, 1941

With Britain's isolation, the German propaganda war rose to fever pitch in an attempt to demoralize the enemy and avoid further confrontation. If the cartoons produced at the time by Osbert Lancaster and Pont are anything to go by, the British remained unmoved. In 'English Equipment' by Fips, Tommy Atkins fills his pipe with 'illusion' tobacco produced by Duff Cooper, the British Minister of Information, his eyes blinkered by Union Jacks with a Star of David on and unable to smell, speak or hear. The caption reads: 'Seeing and hearing nothing, nothing will disturb him. His mouth is sealed with plaster, a clothes-peg on his nose when all around him stinks. The tobacco produces ecstasy.'

Englische Ausrüstung
Fips, *Der Stürmer*, No 46, 1940

Nichts sehen und nichts hören, es tät ja doch nur stören. Ein Pflaster auf das Maul. Und stinkt es ringsum faul, ein Zwicker auf die Nase. Der Tabak gibt Ekstase.

51

For deceiving Nazi dive-bombers as to the centre of gravity

W Heath Robinson, *Heath Robinson at War*, London, 1942

'I don't know what to do with Catchpole, sir: he just keeps smiling through'

Paul Crum

Having observed the manner in which the Nazis had conducted their *Blitzkrieg* invasions on the mainland of Europe, the British were on full alert for signs of disguised enemy parachutists and fifth columnists already working in their midst. Unfortunately, this led to the internment of many innocent foreign nationals, including vehement anti-Nazis (among them cartoonists like Joseph Flatter) who would have willingly served with the Allied armed forces. Fear of German invasion also led, in May 1940, to the formation of the Local Defence Volunteers (later renamed the Home Guard) comprising men either too old, or too young for conscription, or unable to enlist for other reasons. As the cartoon by Nicolas Bentley (1907-78) jokes, the effectiveness of such a group against determined German paratroops might well leave something to be desired (note also the antiquated shotgun – at first the Home Guard were very short of weapons). Fougasse (*below right*), cleverly combines the theme of fuel rationing with invasion fears in his cartoon from *Sorry – No Rubber*, which also alludes to the fact that crossroad direction signs were removed at this time for security reasons.

Far right: Anyone who has experienced RSMs will appreciate the retort in the cartoon by Ronald Searle (b. 1920).

Above left: W Heath Robinson (1872-1944) had gained a high reputation both before and during World War I with his crazy machine drawings in the *Sketch* and *Bystander*. His inventive pen continued its activity in World War II, as this masterful cartoon, from *Heath Robinson at War*, bears witness.

Below left: The joke by 'Paul Crum', in reality Roger Pettiward (1906-42), alludes to Vera Lynn's popular wartime song 'We'll meet again'. Pettiward who, with Pont, was greatly admired as an artist, was killed leading a commando raid at Dieppe.

But, Sergeant, I *am* a ruddy poet
Ronald Searle, *London Opinion*, June 1941

'Eh?'
Nicolas Bentley, *Animal, Vegetable and South Kensington*, London, 1940

'Can you tell me the way to Exminster?'
'How do I know you're not a Fifth Columnist or something?'
'Well, even if I am, you wouldn't want me to waste petrol, would you?'
Fougasse, *Sorry – No Rubber*, London, 1942

Fall to fall description

H B Armstrong, *Melbourne Argus*, 15 August 1940

Royal Air Farce!

Bogner, *Das Schwarze Korps*, 3 October 1940

The necessary prelude to Hitler's 'Operation Sealion' – the projected invasion of Britain – was to win the mastery of the air. However, the Luftwaffe's shortage of long-range fighters and heavy bombers severely limited its effectiveness. These factors – coupled with the development of radar, the highly maneuverable Vickers Supermarine Spitfire, and the fact that pilots fighting over their own country can be quickly returned to the battle if shot down – proved decisive in Britain's 'finest hour.' Victory was later assured when Goering switched his attack from the fighter bases to the cities, thus allowing the RAF forces to regroup. His frustration is well depicted in Shepard's drawing *(right)*. The German version of events, however, reads somewhat differently, as Bogner's feature 'The last reserves of this "royal" air force,' in the reproduction from the front page of the German SS weekly *(opposite)* shows. An anxious Churchill stands amongst his shattered RAF letting off potato (Colorado) beetles as a desperate last measure. The contrast is also rather interesting between Armstrong's cricketing British Lion swiping at the Luftwaffe on eagles' wings and Bogner's broken-down version, held up only by a balloon and still grasping its Colorado beetles in its injured paws *(above)*.

The rock and the storm

E H Shepard, *Punch*, 25 September 1940

54

Einzelpreis 15 Rpf.
zuzüglich ortsüblichem Bestellgeld — Ausland mit ermäßigtem Porto 25 Pf., übriges Ausland 35 Pf.

Berlin, 26. September 1940
39. Folge + 6. Jahrgang

Das Schwarze Korps

ZEITUNG DER SCHUTZSTAFFELN DER NSDAP
Organ der Reichsführung ℠

Verlag: Franz Eher Nachf. GmbH., Zweigniederlassung Berlin Berlin SW 68, Zimmerstraße 88. Fernruf: 11 00 22. Postscheckkonto: Berlin 4454. Anschrift der Schriftleitung: Berlin SW 68, Zimmerstraße 88—91. Anzeigenpreise laut ausliegender Preisliste

Bezugspreise: Durch die Post bei freier Zustellung ins Haus durch den Briefträger 66 Pf., durch Streifband monatlich 95 Pf., Ausland mit ermäßigtem Porto 80 Pf., übriges Ausland RM. 1,05. — In Groß-Berlin erfolgt Zustellung durch Austräger unserer Zweigstellen.

Keine falschen Zukunftsträume

Vor dem Kriege waren die Blicke des deutschen Menschen ins Reichsinnere gerichtet. Es gab und gibt hier hinreichend viele Probleme, deren Lösung uns vollauf beschäftigen kann. Aber der Krieg, den Englands Überheblichkeit vom Zaune brach, stellt uns vor Aufgaben von weltweitem Ausmaß.

Deutschland und Italien haben nicht nur das neue Europa zu formen, sie werden auch vor der Notwendigkeit stehen, die Hinterlassenschaften der abgewirtschafteten Plutokratien auf dem afrikanischen Erdteil neu zu ordnen.

Die Erfüllung dieses geschichtlichen Auftrags fällt räumlich und zeitlich zusammen mit der vom Führer seit jeher betriebenen und geforderten Rückkehr unserer alten deutschen Kolonien. So gehört es zum Ablauf der Dinge, daß die gedankliche, vorbereitende Beschäftigung mit kolonialen Fragen im deutschen Volke um sich greift.

Zuviel Romantik

Wir sagen: im deutschen Volke. Denn selbstverständlich ist für einen Teil des deutschen Volkes das Kolonialproblem die Lebensfrage schlechthin; für jenen Teil nämlich, der schon vor dem Weltkriege ruhmreiche koloniale Arbeit leistete oder nach dem Weltkrieg bemüht war, unter der Herrschaft der fremden „Mandatäre" die Versailler Zwischenperiode schlecht und recht zu überbrücken. Aber diese unsere „Afrikaner" blieben doch stets eine abgesonderte Gruppe, an deren Leistungen, Nöten und Hoffnungen das Volk in seiner Gesamtheit nur geringen Anteil nahm.

Die Jugend mochte sich an den Taten der großen Pioniere, an den herrlichen Leistungen der Schutztruppe im Weltkrieg begeistern. Es war doch nur das romantische Abenteuer, dem ihr Interesse wie ihre Sehnsucht galt. Ein sachliches Denken in imperialen Räumen hatten wir Deutschen noch nicht gelernt. Dazu war unsere afrikanische Tradition zu kurzlebig und unsere persönliche Verflechtung mit den Kolonien zu gering.

Unter hundert deutschen Familien gab es kaum eine, die durch einen eigenen Sproß Beziehungen zu den deutschen Kolonialgebieten unterhalten hätte. Dazu kam, daß ja der alte Kaiserstaat koloniale Probleme nicht anders als eben konnte. Die deutsche Erschließung der Kolonien geschah eben doch nach den Bedürfnissen und Möglichkeiten des Welthandels und blieb damit eine Angelegenheit der unmittelbar interessierten Kreise. Wirklich volkstümlich war sie nicht, denn es war ja auch niemand da, der einen politisch uneinigen, unreifen und uninteressierten Volk stets die volkspolitische Notwendigkeit deutschen kolonialen Schaffens hätte verdeutlichen können.

Heute aber beschäftigt sich unser Volk nicht nur mit den wirtschaftlich-sachlichen Möglichkeiten, die der deutsche Kolonialbesitz eröffnet, es sieht nicht nur die handgreiflichen Vorteile für die Rohstoffwirtschaft und damit für den eigenen Verbrauch, es weiß auch, daß ein Staat mit der Leistungskraft und der ungeheuerlichen Initiative des nationalsozialistischen Deutschlands hier anders zupacken wird als sein Vorgänger. Es weiß, daß der Nationalsozialismus auch diese Probleme vom Volke her und für das Volk wird lösen wollen und daß er gar nicht daran denkt, hier etwa eine Allerweltsweltwirtschaft aus marxistischem Vorzeichen zu betreiben, die wiederum nur wenige Interessentenkreise berühren würde.

Dazu kommt, daß uns das verbündete und weltanschaulich so nahe verwandte Italien das Beispiel einer durch einen autoritär geführten Staat in großen Zügen betriebenen Kolonisation zu bieten scheint. Was in Libyen und Äthiopien geleistet wird, ist so augenfällig großartig, daß es zahllosen Deutschen auf den Fingern brennt, desgleichen zu tun und den Segen deutscher Schaffensfreude und Organisationskunst über weite Räume des schwarzen Erdteils auszubreiten.

Aber das deutsche Volk bleibt bei aller Tatkraft und bei aller Fähigkeit, jedes Problem mit nüchternster Sachlichkeit anzupacken, wenn erst das Signal zum Beginnen gegeben ist, doch ein romantisches Volk. Wir dürften kaum fehlgehen, wenn wir sagen, daß unter hundert Deutschen, die bereit sind oder bereit wären, ihr künftiges Leben kolonialer Arbeit zu widmen, nur zehn oder zwanzig die Möglichkeiten des Erwerbs und des sozialen Aufstiegs nach kaufmännischer Art „kalkuliert" haben.

Die übergroße Mehrheit denkt weniger an sich; sie denkt an die Überwindung räumlicher Enge, an das berauschende Lebensgefühl der unendlichen Weite, sie empfindet die Freude am Aufbauen mit möglichst sichtbarem Erfolg; sie möchte einmal den Schöpfer spielen und Wüsten in fruchtbares Land verwandeln. Wohl denkt sie nicht mehr an das „Abenteuer" im längst entzauberten Urwald. Wohl liegt es dem Deutschen nicht, vom Nichtstun unter Palmen und lachenden Himmel zu träumen. Wohl gründet sich auch diese neue Kolonialromantik auf die Vorstellung, daß man für Deutschland leben, arbeiten und sich opfern würde. Es ist eine Romantik mit durchaus nationalem Vorzeichen. Aber man muß doch prüfen, ob sie nicht etwa falsche Hoffnungen erweckt.

Kein Volksüberschuß

Eine Kolonialpolitik kann immer nur eine unsentimentale und nüchterne Politik sein. Die Tatsachen, von denen eine deutsche Kolonialpolitik auszugehen hat, sind ausschließlich die sachlichen Bedürfnisse des Deutschen Reiches und Volkes.

Wir erstreben mit unseren Kolonien nicht irgendein sagenhaftes Thule, in dem sich Tatkraft und Unternehmungsgeist der deutschen Jugend bewähren könnte. Wir brauchen die Rohstoffquellen, die uns bisher versagt waren, zur Ernährung und Bekleidung des deutschen Volkes, zur Beschäftigung unserer verarbeitenden Industrie, zur Hebung und Sicherung jener Lebenshaltung, auf die der deutsche Mensch nach seiner Leistung Anspruch erheben darf. Die Kolonien können daher niemals Selbstzweck sein, und man darf niemals den Fehler begehen, ihre Probleme losgelöst von denen des Mutterlandes zu betrachten.

Die Frage, die neben der Rohstoffbeschaffung in den kommenden Aufbaujahren uns das größte Kopfzerbrechen verursachen wird, ist zweifellos das Problem der Arbeitskraft. Sie fehlt uns heute schon an allen Ecken und Enden, sie wird uns morgen erst recht fehlen. Gingen vor 1933 nicht wenige Deutsche in die unter fremder Mandatsherrschaft stehenden Kolonien, weil das Mutterland ihnen das Recht auf Arbeit versagte, so hat sich diese seinerzeitige Triebfeder der Abwanderung in die Kolonien ins Gegenteil verkehrt:

Der Kräftebedarf des Mutterlandes ist ein Magnet, der immer bestrebt sein wird, möglichst viele, möglichst alle Kräfte festzuhalten. Dieser Magnet führt heute schon unzählige Fremdstämmige aus dem europäischen Osten und Südosten ins Reich, und auch diese Entwicklung wird anhalten und zunehmen in dem Ausmaß, in dem der deutsche Lebensstandard sich hebt und der ungelernte deutsche Arbeiter immer seltener wird.

Würden wir größere Menschenmassen an die Kolonien abgeben, würden wir in den Kolonien — wie man sich das in den Jahren der widernatürlichen „Krise" vorstellte — Gebiete zur Unterbringung eines „Bevölkerungsüberschusses" erblicken, so müßte das zu einer höchst bedenklichen und unerwünschten Entwicklung führen:

Die besten, unternehmungslustigsten, tüchtigsten deutschen Menschen würden das Mutterland verlassen und würden in die Kolonien gehen; und in die Lücken, die sie hinterlassen, müßten Fremdstämmige einrücken, die wir doch stets nur als Gäste und keinesfalls als Ersatz für deutsches Blut bei uns sehen wollen. Deutschland kolonisierte Afrika, und der Osten und Südosten würde am Ende Deutschland kolonisieren!

Unser „koloniales Denken" muß sich daher grundsätzlich der Tatsache beugen, daß im Gegensatz zu allen anderen Staaten und im Gegensatz zu unserer eigenen Vergangenheit das nationalsozialistische Deutschland jedenfalls keinen Bevölkerungsüberschuß abgeben kann, weil es ihn gar nicht besitzt. Ganz im Gegenteil! Wir fördern mit allen Mitteln die Vermehrung der Geburten. Wir könnten heute statt der 85 Millionen gut und gerne deren 100 gebrauchen und wären um ihre Beschäftigung und um die altgewöhnliche Sicherung ihres Daseins nicht verlegen. Das und nichts anderes sollte der Preis unseres Sieges sein.

Nüchterne Tatsachen

Wir brauchen unsere Kolonien, um das Leben und die Arbeit dieser Millionenmassen im Reiche selbst zu sichern, nicht aber als zusätzlichen Wohn- und Siedlungsraum. Wer sich demnach ein deutsches Kolonialreich als ein anderes, zweites Deutschland unter heißerer Sonne vorstellt, wer unterm Äquator deutsche Städte und Dörfer aufblühen sieht, ist nur ein Schwärmer, er hegt selbst oder erweckt in anderen nur falsche Hoffnungen.

Unsere Arbeit in den Kolonien muß darauf abgestellt sein, mit möglichst geringem Menscheneinsatz den höchstmöglichen Nutzen für das Mutterland zu erzielen. Nicht der deutsche Siedler, Bauer, Handwerker, der in den neuen Heimat Wurzeln schlägt, wird das Gesicht der deutschen Kolonien prägen, sondern der deutsche Verwalter, der als Organisator im landwirtschaftlichen, forstwirtschaftlichen, bergbaulichen, industriellen, kaufmännischen wie verkehrstechnischen Sektor als Beauftragter der Heimat,

Das letzte Aufgebot...
... dieser „königlichen" Luftwaffe

Zeichnung: Bogner

His Lordship's remarks should be quite interesting when he sees this little lot, Cooper

Carl Giles, *Reynolds News*, 17 November 1940

**'Well, I must be toddling in now.
I mustn't miss the 9 o'clock news'**

Joe Lee, *Evening News*, 1940

'Three hundred and seventy-six, three hundred and seventy-seven, three hundred and seventy-eight. Swastikas as plain as pikestaffs'

Pont, *Punch*, 25 September 1940

The civilians' view of the Battle of Britain is well illustrated in this group of cartoons. The drawing by Joe Lee (1902-74) from his 'Smiling Through' series for the *Evening News* typifies the general attitude then prevalent. Giles's cartoon takes the war into the homes of the aristocracy, while the brilliant Pont drawing, complete with unperturbed cats playing under the deckchairs, is a classic of its kind.

Ein Mörder betet!

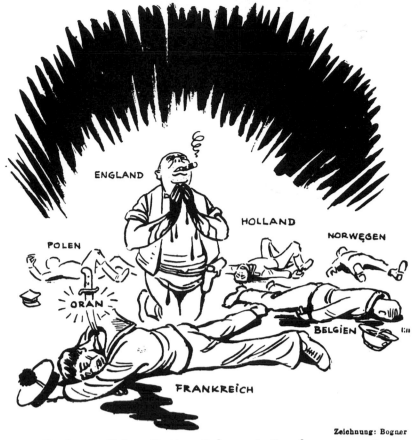

ENGLAND

POLEN

HOLLAND

NORWEGEN

ORAN

BELGIEN

FRANKREICH

Zeichnung: Bogner

Und nun, lieber Gott, sei _du_ mein Bundesgenosse!

Bogner, *Das Schwarze Korps*, 18 July 1940

With the fall of France, Britain was anxious lest the powerful French Mediterranean Fleet should fall into Axis hands, and was prepared to take extreme measures to ensure that it did not. The attack on 3 July 1940 by the Royal Navy's Force H on the Algerian ports of Oran and Mers-el-Kebir, after the French had refused to surrender their ships, led to the loss of nearly 1300 French lives. Not surprisingly, the Germans made much of this act. In Bogner's powerful cartoon 'A murderer prays,' the bloody-handed Churchill, surrounded by the corpses of Norway, Holland, Belgium and Poland, kneels over the body of a French sailor with the words: 'And now, dear God, *you* can be my ally!' The duplicity of the French government under Pétain's pro-Nazi Vichy regime is the subject of Zec's cartoon. The West African town of Dakar was unsuccessfully attacked by British and Free French forces on 23 September 1940 in an effort to capture the port and the remaining battleships of the French fleet – notably the *Richelieu*.

Saving France – for Germany

Philip Zec, *Daily Mirror*, 11 October 1940

As a protection from bombs and falling masonry during the 'Blitz,' do-it-yourself shelters were distributed to the public. The earliest version was the Anderson shelter, named after the Home Secretary, consisting of a tubular dome of corrugated steel half-buried in the ground. Strube's 'little man' is more concerned for his prize marrow than his family's welfare (*right*). Herbert Morrison, who took over from Anderson in October 1940, lent his name to an indoor shelter which resembled a heavily built wire box, satirized below by W A Sillince (1906-74). But a large proportion of the population preferred to sleep in the Underground stations. In Low's 'London sleeps,' Colonel Blimp addresses Sir John Anderson and Low himself. (Lord Beaverbrook was Minister for Aircraft Production at this time.)

London sleeps

David Low, *Evening Standard*, 24 September 1940

'Is it all right now, Henry?' 'Yes, not even scratched.'

Sidney Strube, *Daily Express*, November 1940

'By the way, did you remember to feed the canary?'

W A Sillince, *Punch*, 28 May 1941

**Uncle Frederic at 8.32 p.m. last Tuesday – if his description
is strictly in accordance with the facts**
Pont, *Punch*, 27 November 1940

**'Oh, Mr Butterfield, Mr Fitzsimmonds would like
to see you in his office at once'**
David Langdon, *Punch*, 12 February 1941

Above: Beneath the bombs, business in London and the blitzed cities went on as well as the limitations on transport and communications and the survival of offices and shops allowed. In defiance of the German attacks, Union Flags began to appear in the rubble to show that the British spirit was not broken. The absurdity of the drawing by David Langdon (b. 1914) was perhaps not so far from the truth in many cases, though, as Pont's cartoon shows, there was a tendency to embellish the facts somewhat. (Note 'F P' for Frederic Pont on briefcase.) L H Siggs' bridge-players *(right)* are a study in British sang-froid (Brest was the heavily fortified submarine base on the French coast).

'Dummy pops off and attacks the Docks at Brest – OK?'
L H Siggs, *Punch*, 27 August 1941

LE PEINTRE

SON ŒUVRE

André François, *Marianne*, n.d.

Otto Soglow, *New Yorker War Album*, London, 1943

Right: Japan joined the Axis powers of Germany and Italy by signing the Tripartite Pact on 27 September 1940. The Pact stated that all member countries would declare war on any other power which attacked any one of them (though, interestingly, relations with the Soviet Union were not included). The illustration of the event by Partridge has a mocking tone, comparing the three nations to the three monkeys who hear no evil, see no evil and speak no evil. The trio are up in the clouds on a gnarled tree branch looking at no one but themselves. André Farkas, better known as André François, was born in Rumania in 1915. His cartoon (*above left*) 'The painter and his work' alludes to Hitler's early art-school training in Austria. Otto Soglow (1900-75), a New Yorker, contributed drawings to many US magazines post 1925.

Tripartite Pact

'Hear no good!' 'See no good!' 'Speak no good!'
Bernard Partridge, *Punch*, 9 October 1940

Back to the wall
Clive Uptton, *Daily Sketch*, 1940

WC der neue Gott der Griechen

Der alte Zeus ward einst zum Stier weil er verstrickt in Eros Schlingen, und die Verwandlung tat gelingen, Damit Europa er entführ. Doch einem Rindvieh macht's Beschwerden, nun umgekehrt zum Gott zu werden.

Fips, *Der Stürmer*, No 47, 1940

Eager to match the Nazi successes in northern Europe, and confident following the earlier Italian campaigns in Ethiopia and Albania, Mussolini decided to mount a full-scale invasion of Greece via Albania. But he found himself strongly opposed by Greek forces who, aided by the British, not only repulsed the attack but drove the Italians a considerable distance back into Albania. The cartoon by Clive Uptton owes something to Low's 'Very well, alone,' but still packs considerable power. Perhaps needless to say, the Germans were far from pleased with the performance of their Axis partner but begrudgingly awarded the victory to Churchill, as shown in the Fips cartoon, 'WC the new god of the Greeks.' Note the sign pointing to Olympus and the WC and whisky flask – both frequently used as props to attack Winston Churchill, who was known to like whisky.

For Britain and its allies, the military situation during most of 1941 was grim. The defeat of the Italians in Greece and at Cape Matapan were a boost to Allied morale until the Germans counterattacked in the Mediterranean, driving the Allies off the European mainland on the northern shore and back to Alexandria on the southern. In the Battle of the Atlantic, Germany progressively gained the upper hand, with 1229 Allied ships sunk in this year. However, Hitler's decision to invade the Soviet Union in June, coupled with increasing military aid granted to the Allies by the United States, gave a glimmer of hope.

Meanwhile, the United States was being drawn into confrontation with Japan in the Pacific. Embargoes on oil exports to Japan effectively reduced her supplies by 90 percent. General Tojo became Japanese premier in October and the militarists now dictated the country's foreign policy. On 7 December, Japan carried out a devastating attack on the United States Pacific Fleet at Pearl Harbor. Then Germany declared war on the United States. A true world war had begun. With the industrial might of the United States ranged against them, Japan, Germany and Italy now faced an arduous task. In taking on both the Soviet Union and the United States, they had made a fatal error of judgement.

Right: A classic situation-comedy cartoon by the American master of the genre, Peter Arno. Arno (1904-68), whose real name was Curtis Arnoux Peters, came from a wealthy New York family. He changed his name when he dropped out of Yale and began making a living first as a jazz musician and then as a writer and cartoonist for such publications as the *New Yorker, Harper's Bazaar* and *Saturday Evening Post*. The British soldiers in this cartoon are perfectly positioned in the picture for the eye to follow the disappearing column.

'It feels like it might be a grain of sand'
Peter Arno, *New Yorker War Album*, London, 1943

On 9 December 1940 the Western Desert Force of British, Indian, Australian, New Zealand and South African troops under the command of Major-General O'Connor attacked the Italian positions in North Africa. In two days they had captured Sidi Barrani and by 9 February 1941 had driven the Italians out of Egypt and advanced deep into Libya itself, capturing the fortress of Bardia and the key port of Tobruk. In two months 130,000 Italian prisoners were taken by a much smaller Allied force for the cost of 555 Allied lives. 'An Egyptian freeze,' in imitation of Egyptian temple decorations, shows Graziani, the head of the Italian

forces in North Africa, desperately requesting reinforcements and supplies. Mussolini plans to sack him like former chief-of-staff Badoglio – who had been forced to resign after the Italian débâcle in Greece – while to the lower right German Foreign Minister Ribbentrop shows his displeasure by poking his Italian counterpart, Count Ciano, in the face (Graziani was in fact replaced on 12 February).

The unexpectedly fast retreat of the Italians in the face of the surprise attack is shown in Low's illustration of the Churchill quotation (the Australian kangaroo well to the front).

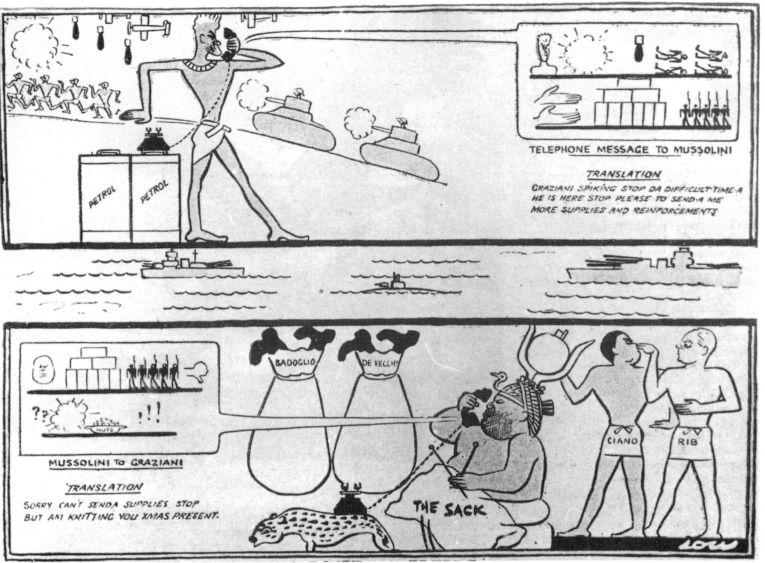

An Egyptian freeze

David Low, *Evening Standard*, 1941

'We are now getting into our stride' – Churchill

David Low, *Evening Standard*, 27 January 1941

Until December 1941, the United States was ambivalent in its attitude toward the conflict in Europe and North Africa. A vocal lobby pleaded for isolation from affairs many thousands of miles away. President Roosevelt, however, was keen to aid Britain by any means short of war. In his famous 'fireside chat' broadcast to the people on 29 December 1940, the president declared that the United States must become the great 'arsenal of democracy' and by 11 March 1941 the Lend-Lease Act had become law, allowing the Allies to 'borrow' as much military equipment as they liked without cash payment. Strube's 'little man' warms himself at the Roosevelt hearth (*opposite top*) as Hitler and Goering look on in consternation outside. Illingworth's American Eagle, in place of the usual stork, delivers urgently required arms across the Atlantic as Liberty lights the way and guides the convoys below. The Axis view paints the same picture but with a different twist: John Bull (in flames) is indeed receiving help from America as Germany and Italy stand astride Europe, but a nervous Uncle Sam has caught sight of a sentinel Japan to his rear while his gifts lie burning in the sea, the victims of U-boat wolf-packs.

The way of a stork
Leslie Illingworth, *Punch*, 29 January 1941

Axis leaflet, c1941

Roosevelt's Fireside Chat
Sidney Strube, *Daily Express*, 3 January 1941

On 10 May 1941 Hitler's deputy, Rudolf Hess, single-handedly flew an Me 110 to Britain and parachuted to earth near Glasgow in the Lowlands of Scotland. For some considerable time his claims to be Hess were dismissed out of hand. When his identity was verified, he was made a prisoner of war. The Russians later became convinced that Hess's mission had been to persuade the British royal family, some of whom were believed to have pro-Nazi feelings, to make a separate peace with Germany and join in the war against the Soviet Union. The cartoon by Low (*below*) alludes to the fact that the Germans immediately disowned Hess as a madman (he was replaced by Martin Bormann).

'He must have been mad'
David Low, *Evening Standard*, 15 May 1941

Right: The oath Goering made was that no enemy bombs would ever fall on Berlin. If they did, he said, 'You can call me Meyer' (a Jewish name). Considerable mileage was made of this boast by the Allies when the RAF raided the German capital on the nights of 24-29 August 1940. Adolf Hoffmeister (1902-73) was a Czech artist who fled when the Nazis came to power but continued to produce political cartoons in exile. Arriving first in France, he was captured and put in a concentration camp when the Germans overran the country in 1940. He then escaped to Casablanca, was imprisoned by the Vichy regime there, escaped to Spain, was imprisoned by the Franco regime and finally escaped to the United States, via Havana, in 1941. (The part of Victor Lazlo in the film *Casablanca* is supposed to be based on Hoffmeister.)

Below: The loss of much of the Italian Fleet at Taranto in November 1940 and at the Battle of Cape Matapan (26-29 March 1941) was a severe blow to the Axis, particularly as the German Kriegsmarine was considerably under strength and command of the Mediterranean was vital to maintain supply-lines to troops in North Africa. Hitler's displeasure is evident in the picture from the cover of Stephen Roth's book *Divided They Fall*, where the Italian Navy weighs heavier on the scales than fish-out-of-water Mussolini. In Kem's Christmas card (subtitled, 'Mare . . . monstrum'), produced for his friends in December 1941, the incompetent donkey Benito (from a series of cartoons entitled 'Adolf and his Donkey Benito') manages to scramble on to some wreckage, his trident broken and with an amputated leg and damaged ear, looking very doleful indeed. ('Mare Nostrum,' or 'our sea,' was how the Fascists liked to regard the Mediterranean.)

Goering's oath
Adolf Hoffmeister, *Jesters in Earnest*, London, 1940

Stephen Roth, *Divided They Fall* (cover), London, 1943

Kem, Christmas card, December 1941

Edgar Longman, Greek poster, c1941

After the failure of the Italian invasion of Greece, Hitler decided to launch his own all-out attack, Operation Marita. To this end he forced the Bulgarians to agree to allow the passage of his troops up to the Greek border. However, a similar agreement forced upon Prince Paul of Yugoslavia was violently disrupted when Paul was overthrown in a military *coup d'état* led by the Serbian General Simovic. This turnabout precipitated a full-scale German offensive against Yugoslavia on 6 April 1941. The Yugoslav armies were destroyed within a week. In Greece the Germans smashed through the Metaxas Line and by 27 April were in Athens. The Allies evacuated 50,000 troops to Crete and the Greek prime minister committed suicide.

The Greek poster 'Get out of Greece' has an inspiring though perhaps futile message: the Nazi monster is just too big to be stopped by this flesh wound.

Battle for Britain – Part 2
David Low, *Evening Standard*, 25 July 1941

Left: One of Low's most reproduced cartoons was occasioned by the improvements to the air defense of Britain by the introduction of radar.

Harvest Moon
David Low, *Evening Standard*, 9 May 1941

Na twee Jaar
Pouwels, *Storm SS*, 5 September 1941

Operation Barbarossa, the German invasion of the Soviet Union, began at 0300 hours on 22 June 1941. By noon the same day the Soviet Air Force had lost 1200 planes and by 9 July 300,000 prisoners had been taken at Minsk. The speed of the Nazi advance was phenomenal: on 12 July Moscow was bombed, on 5 August 310,000 surrendered at Smolensk, on 15 September Leningrad was isolated and under siege, on the 19th Kiev fell at the cost of 500,000 Soviet prisoners, three weeks later 650,000 were captured at Vyazma and by 15 November Moscow itself was at risk. Russian caricaturists made much of this sudden betrayal by the Nazis, as the poster (*overleaf*) by the Kukryniksi group shows. Behind the cheerful mask the odious-featured, gun-toting Hitler claws his way through the Nazi-Soviet Pact document to be confronted by a Soviet bayonet. Allied reactions, meanwhile, were mixed. Some people were relieved that the main thrust of the German attack had now switched to the Eastern Front, as Low's cutting drawing proves (*top left*). The cartoon by Pouwels (*above*), in the Dutch SS newspaper *Storm SS*, depicts the state of the war after two years with considerable confidence. Published in early September it shows the German war machine crushing Stalin before moving on to bury Churchill (note the German propaganda motif of a whisky bottle) in a hole marked 'London.'

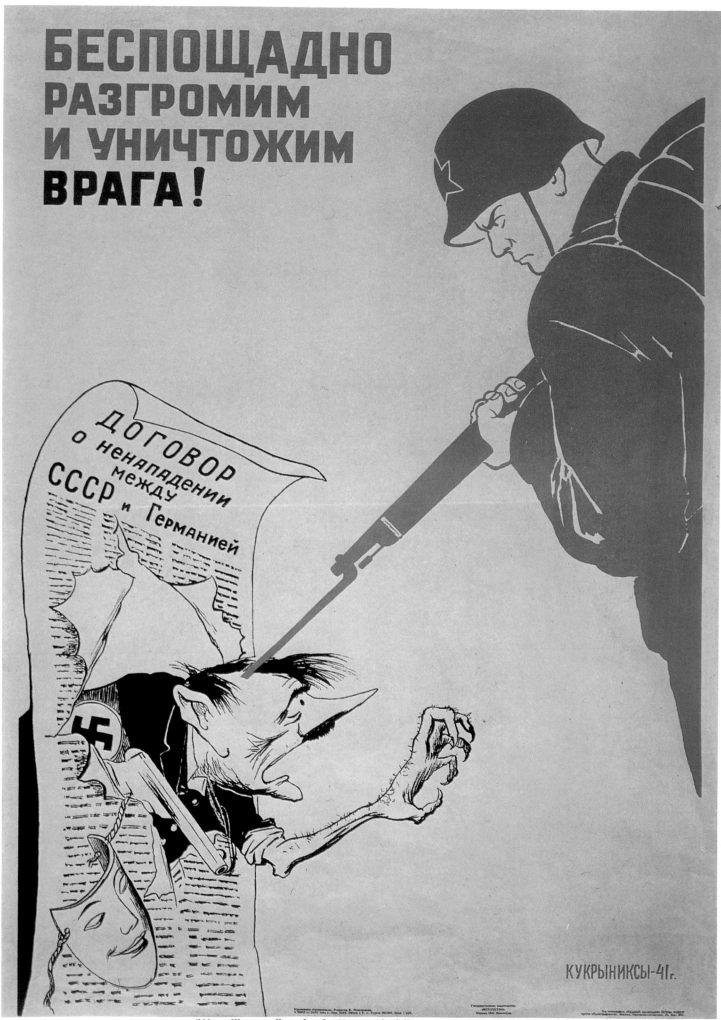

'We will mercilessly shatter and obliterate the enemy'
Kukryniksi, Soviet poster, 1941

'Napoleon suffered defeat and so will the conceited Hitler'
Kukryniksi, Soviet poster, 1941

The initial success of the German Army in the Soviet Union gave the Nazis much to crow about, but by December 1941 the Russians' most reliable weapon, winter, was beginning to hit the enemy hard. As with Napoleon over a century before, the aggressors would have to face up to Generals January and February. The powerful Kukryniksi poster (*above*) has Hitler retreating holding the torn-up Nazi-Soviet Pact, the shadows behind telling the similar story of Napoleon's defeat in 1812.

Arthur Szyk's splendid cover for *Collier's* (right) has Hitler looking worried, his chips dwindling as Death, in an old German uniform, looks on. In his hand he holds only three jokers: Mussolini, Pétain and Tojo, while his puppets, lifeless on the floor, can offer little help. Russia, by contrast, has the blackjack winners, the United States and Great Britain (the V for Victory sign also appears across the top of the cards in Morse Code).

Arthur Szyk, *Collier's* (cover), 1 November 1941

The German advance on Moscow (Operation Typhoon), was finally halted on 5 December 1941 and the following day the Red Army under Marshal Zhukov counterattacked. Lacking proper winter clothing and with inadequate supplies for a winter campaign the Germans were now in an uncomfortable position. Furious with his generals, who advised a tactical withdrawal to begin a fresh offensive in the spring, Hitler took personal command of the German Army on 19 December and urged the troops to stand firm. Boris Efimov (b. 1900), whose work was much admired by David Low, has the cold and snivelling schoolboy Hitler overshadowed by schoolmaster Napoleon (who was in reality a very small man), while Mussolini, whose scars bear witness to an earlier 'history lesson,' cowers in fear. (The gruesome 'Maneater' poster [*right*] reveals a less subtle side to Efimov's art.) In Vicky's cartoon, set in a pagan temple, Goebbels offers the army to be sacrificed by Nordic god-figure Hitler on the altar of Nazism while the sheeplike German people look on.

At the history lesson
Boris Efimov, 1941

Moscow aftermath
Vicky, *News Chronicle*, 23 December 1941

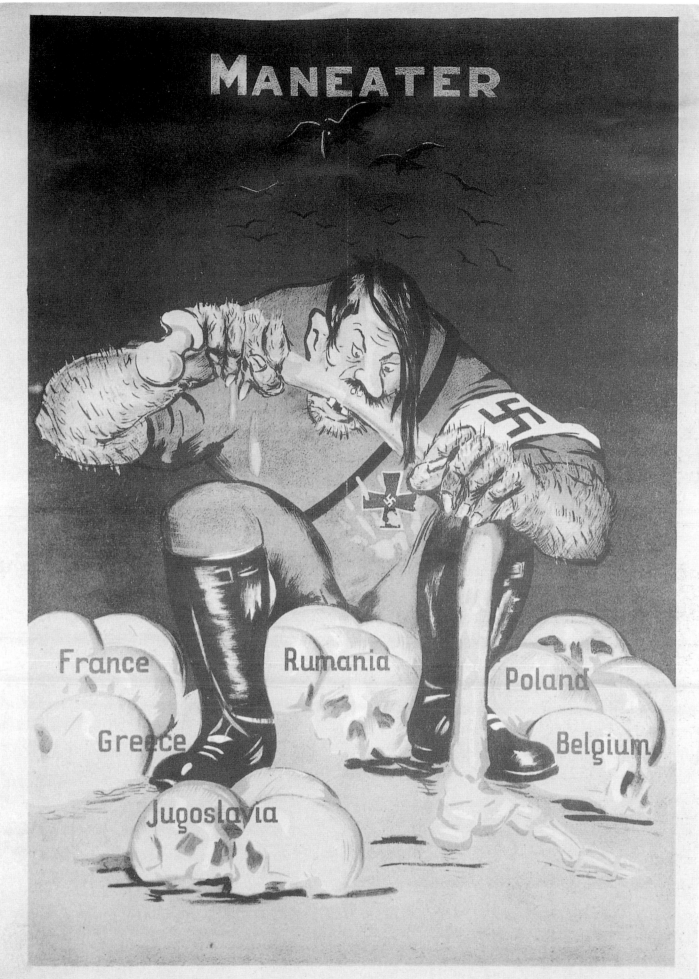

Boris Efimov, Soviet poster, 1941

Arthur Szyk, *Collier's* (cover), 12 December 1942

KARİKATÜR

Two contrasting views of Franklin D Roosevelt during his presidency. The confident smiling Roosevelt exuding bonhomie and benevolent power and smoking a Tojo pipe on the cover of the Turkish magazine, *Karikatür*, is in direct opposition to Kondo's green-faced, Dracula-fanged grasping monster. *Manga*, the official wartime cartoon magazine of Japan, dished out similar treatment to Churchill and Stalin. Hidezo Kondo (1908-79) was very much the elder statesman of Japanese cartooning.

Ramiz, *Karikatür* (cover), 7 October 1943

The sudden attack by Japanese carrier-based aircraft on the US Pacific Fleet moored in Pearl Harbor, Hawaii, on Sunday 7 December 1941 completely stunned the United States and the rest of the world. In the words of President Roosevelt, it was 'a date which will live in infamy.' In less than 30 minutes a large proportion of the United States' largest fleet had been destroyed. The immediate effect of the raid was to rally a divided America into a declaration of war on Japan the following day. On 11 December Germany and Italy declared war on the United States and World War II became truly global.

Arthur Szyk shows a gruesome vampire bat hovering over Hawaii, in the first anniversary *Collier's* cover.

Hidezo Kondo, *Manga* (cover), 1943

**'If you want to know who we are.
We are gentlemen of Japan'**
Rea Irvin, *New Yorker War Album*, London 1943

Left: A view of the Pearl Harbor raid. Irvin spoofs on the opening lines of Gilbert and Sullivan's *The Mikado* as the 'Nazi' Japanese in their national costume perform a grisly dance of destruction. (Rea Irvin [1881-1972] had considerable influence on US cartoon art and, as well as being art editor of the *New Yorker*, created the famous cover design for that magazine.)

La maschera e il volto

La Presidentessa – 'Ehi, Delano! Ti sei dimenticato la maschera!'
Barbara, *Marc' Aurelio*, 1941

With the passing of the Lend-Lease Act in March 1941 and the United States' increasing involvement in the war, a spate of anti-American cartoons appeared in the Axis press. The emphasis was generally anti-Semitic – particularly as a considerable number of Jewish refugees from Europe had settled in New York and elsewhere in the country – though attacks on American expansionism and decadence were also common. 'The mask and the face' (*above*) presents an Italian view of America: 'The First Lady: "Hey Delano! You forgot your mask" – the true face of the Jewish plutocrat being revealed to the public. In the cartoon by Pouwels for *Storm SS*, New York becomes 'Jew York' and the Statue of Liberty becomes a Jew holding a cashbook while the grim reaper passes Roosevelt who shouts: 'If Germany wins *our* freedom will be lost.'

New-York werd Jew-York
Roosevelt – 'Als Duitschland wint, is *onze* vrijheid verloren'
Pouwels, *Storm SS*, 6 June 1941

77

Robert and Philip Spence, *Struwwelhitler*, London, n.d.

Two versions of Heinrich Hoffmann's popular nineteenth-century collection of moral tales, *Struwwelpeter* (1845). In the title tale the boy with unkempt hair and long nails finally learns his lesson when his fingers are cut off with a giant pair of scissors. In the version by the Spence brothers presented to the *Daily Sketch* War Relief Fund, Hitler is seen dishevelled and with bleeding fingers (*Schrecklickheit* is German for 'frightfulness'), while the 'Oistros' edition shows him with elongated nails which turn into swastikas.

Oistros, *Truffle Eater*, London, n.d.

British poster, September 1941

Incendiary bombs caused great havoc in the war on both sides, culminating in the firestorms of Hamburg, Dresden and Tokyo. In Britain the Ministry of Home Security began a campaign in 1941 to make the public aware of the firebomb menace, and 'firewatchers' were stationed on rooftops at night to monitor outbreaks in the cities. Boris Efimov (*right*) manipulates the image to turn Hitler himself into an incendiary about to be extinguished for ever by the Big Three of the Soviet Union on the one hand and the United States and Great Britain on the other.

Disposing of the Fascist incendiary
Boris Efimov, 1942

79

Aircraft identification became a popular craze for civilians, as well as being of supreme importance for the military. Osbert Lancaster's evil-looking urchin (*right*) speaks with a self-confidence that worries his mother and cannot be ignored by his father, who is forced to look up from his newspaper. The series of 'Oddentificatons' (*far right*) by E A C Wren (1908-82) ran in *Aeroplane* magazine in the 1940s. Their popularity has been such that a facsimile edition of the original collection was reprinted in the 1980s. Each anthropomorphic aircraft caricature, together with its rhyming humorous verse, appeared opposite a photograph of the genuine article and a brief description of its history. (The aircraft described in the cartoon shown is the German Focke-Wulf 190 fighter.)

'I know it's a Messerschmitt!'
Osbert Lancaster, *New Pocket Cartoons*, London, 1941

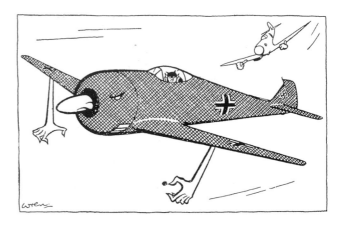

Strange, is it not, how Nazi evil
In outward form can be perceived.
The One-Nine-O's a nasty devil,
Compound of badness unrelieved,
The blackguard scowl, a covert leer,
But underneath a hidden fear—
"Beware, O Hun! Your time is near ! !"

Oddentification
Wren, *Aeroplane*, 1942

Hvert blad sit publikum
Harald Engman, December 1943

Daily life in Nazi-occupied Europe continued despite the presence of the Germans. Apart from active collaborators, society divided into those who begrudgingly accepted their lot, knowing that reprisals would be severe, and those who openly or covertly aided the efforts of resistance fighters, often coordinated by governments in exile in Britain. Giles's Dutch cartoon makes light of a situation that would have dire consequences for the local inhabitants. The 'underground' drawing, 'Every paper has its public', by the Dane Harald Engman (*below left*) has an unknown hand burning holes in and drawing a Star of David on an SS officer's greatcoat. (Note the suitcase filled with dynamite on the floor, the advertisements for the RAF and the fact that the civilians are reading resistance newspapers.)

The anti-government cartoon (*below*) was the last published by the British Communist Party newspaper, the *Daily Worker*, before it was closed down by the Home Secretary, Herbert Morrison, himself a Labour MP. Another issue was in fact printed but was suppressed before distribution.

'Vot you mean – you think you don't know nodding about it!'
Carl Giles, *Reynolds News*, 9 May 1941

Their gallant allies
Chen, *Daily Worker*, 20 January 1941

1942

The Japanese attacks on Pearl Harbor, the Philippines, Hong Kong and Malaya in December 1941 caught the Allies completely off balance. They were poorly prepared to meet the rapid, precisely executed assaults. By April the Dutch East Indies, Burma, Malaya, Singapore, Indonesia and most of the Pacific Islands had fallen, and Australia was directly threatened. In addition, the sinking of *Repulse* and *Prince of Wales* left only three American carriers in the Pacific to combat the vastly superior Japanese Navy and its well-trained naval pilots.

Meanwhile in Europe and North Africa the German advances continued, pushing the Red Army back to Stalingrad in the south and pressuring Moscow and Leningrad in the north, while Rommel crushed all Allied resistance in Libya and Egypt.

However, in June, a significant American naval victory off Midway Island, Hawaii, redressed the balance in the Pacific at a stroke, and by October the Germans had become bogged down in Russia with the prospect of a hard winter ahead. In North Africa too, the Eighth Army, re-equipped and with new commanders (Alexander and Montgomery), drove the Afrika Korps back in November. With American troops pushing eastward from Algeria, after the Torch landings, the Axis forces were progressively squeezed into a pocket in Tunisia.

The tide had begun to turn for the Allies, but there was still a long way to go.

Churchills Silvesterkatzenjammer

„Goddam, wie ist mir mein Lügen- und Illusionspunsch schlecht bekommen!!"

Churchill dopo la sbornia di San Silvestro: "Goddam! . . . Come m'ha fatto male il ponce delle menzogne e delle illusioni!"

Erich Schilling, *Simplicissimus*, 1 January 1942

Munro, *Lahore Civil and Military Gazette*, 1 January 1942

Above and left: Two views of Churchill's attitude to the New Year of 1942. Munro's baby Winston bursting out of a grenade is in stark contrast to Schilling's decrepit old man in 'Churchill's New Year hangover.' The mangy alleycats drinking wine from a tureen, have collars indicating recent disasters: Pearl Harbor, Balkans, Siam, Russia, and the names of the two British war ships recently sunk off Singapore, *Repulse* and *Prince of Wales*. The caption reads: 'Damn, look how my lies-and-illusions punch has been received.' Erich Schilling (1885-1945), formerly anti-Nazi, was later said to be Goebbels' favorite cartoonist.

Opposite: The rapid advance of the Japanese in Malaya and the fall of Singapore gave Australians considerable concern that they would be the next to face Tojo's war machine on their own land. With the attack on Darwin by 150 carrier-based aircraft of the Japanese Navy on 19 February 1942 and the landings on neighbouring New Guinea the following month, alarm bells began to ring. Japanese propaganda leaflets (*top right*) tried to demoralize the 'Diggers' by speculating about the activities of American troops stationed in their homeland. Others (*right*) were aimed at Asians serving with the British.

Japanese aerial leaflet, n.d.

Japanese aerial leaflet, n.d.

In early 1942 Japanese forces pushed down the Malay peninsula. Singapore, whose fortifications were all directed towards the possibility of a seaborne assault, was dangerously exposed. Disorganized and lacking essential supplies, the key British garrison could not hold out. The surrender of the 138,000 troops at Singapore on 15 February 1942 was one of Britain's most ignominious defeats of all time. Low's cartoon neatly encapsulates the confusion that surrounded the affair. The success of the Japanese in Asia was a great fillip to Axis morale and the drawing by Truetsch for the cover of *Das Schwarze Korps* on 12 February shows the British armies being booted out of Malaya and Africa by Japan and Germany. Note the specific naming of Rommel, who was fast becoming a national hero since arriving in Tripoli the year before.

Die Tommies sind wieder überall ins 'Hinter-treffen' geraten
Truetsch, *Das Schwarze Korps*, 12 February 1942

Blimpapore
David Low, *Evening Standard*, 22 January 1942

1942

Sonnenbrand . . . und bald kein Öl mehr!
Bogner, *Das Schwarze Korps*,
23 April 1942

'All our information goes to show that not only are the enemy's lines of communication becoming dangerously extended, but also the treads of his elephants are wearing out.'

Osbert Lancaster, *Daily Express*,
26 March 1942

'I repeat sir, the Japs are no sportsmen – it's always been clearly understood that these jungles are strictly impenetrable'

Osbert Lancaster, *Daily Express*,
20 January 1942

The British were again caught complacent and unprepared when the Japanese stormed into Burma. Indeed, air-raid instruction to the inhabitants of Rangoon was so slack that many civilians stood in the streets as the first wave of Japanese bombers arrived, leading to countless unnecessary deaths. Rangoon fell on 7 March 1942 and Mandalay on 1 May. Osbert Lancaster's cartoons pinpoint the attitudes of the British civil service and Army staff during this period. 'Sunburn . . . and soon no more oil' by Bogner has an exposed John Bull in the Indian Ocean, the sea lanes closing fast as British shipping is sunk, thus denying to the Allies the important Burma oilfields.

Right: The raid on Tokyo by 16 B-25 Mitchell bombers, led by Lieutenant-Colonel Jimmy Doolittle, on 18 April 1942 caused panic among the Japanese. The effect on morale was similar to that of the RAF's attack on Berlin after Goering's boast that no bomb would drop on the German capital. American opinion was outraged when it was learnt that three captured airmen who had bailed out from damaged planes had been tortured and summarily executed by the Japanese. Sy Moyer pulls no punches in this grisly cartoon.

Sy Moyer, 1942

The lesson of Stalingrad
Boris Efimov, 1942

'Wherever a German soldier sets foot, there he will stay'
A Pelc, *Jesters in Earnest*, London, 1943

Halted at Moscow in the north, the German armies none the less continued to advance in the southern republics of the Soviet Union, overrunning the Crimea in July 1942. By 16 September they had reached the suburbs of Stalingrad and begun a siege of the city. However again beset by bad weather and hampered by determined house-to-house fighting by the Russians under General Chuikov, the spearhead force, the Sixth Army under General Paulus, was unable to win the day. After a Soviet counteroffensive begun on 19 November the Sixth Army, comprising 300,000 men, found itself encircled. Manstein's efforts to relieve Paulus by a further attack proved in vain and on 2 February 1943, having been made a Field Marshal by Hitler only the day before, Paulus surrendered – the first German Field Marshal ever to do so.

Efimov's rat-trap (far left) represents the Red Army knocking the stuffing out of Paulus's forces while the floor is littered with imperatives from Hitler to take Stalingrad at all costs – with progressively later dates succeeding the crossed-out ones that begin in August. The caption reads: 'General Paulus takes a practical lesson in Soviet strategy.' The Czech cartoonist Pelc satirizes Hitler's personal command to the German Army to stand fast – corpses do not move. (Of the 300,000 Germans surrounded at Stalingrad, half were killed and 90,000 taken prisoner, the remainder having been evacuated by air. There were three days of national mourning after this military disaster.)

Left: On 16 April 1942 the entire island of Malta was awarded the George Cross – the highest British decoration available to civilians – for its inhabitants' dogged resistance to the intensive bombardment of Goering's Luftwaffe. Situated between Sicily and the coast of Libya, Malta was of vital importance to the Allies. With a secure base on the island the Royal Navy and RAF could harass the essential supply-line between Sicily and the Axis forces in Africa. Goering looks on as his Luftwaffe 'moths' are destroyed in Low's powerful drawing.

Moths and the flame
David Low, *Evening Standard*, 18 May 1942

Der Feind sieht Dein Licht!

Verdunkeln!

German poster, c1942

After the fall of France and before troops could be reassembled for a counter-offensive, the only powerful weapon Britain had left to strike at Germany was the long-range bomber. Once Arthur 'Bomber' Harris took over Bomber Command in early 1942, he pushed for massed attacks on German cities by night. Directed primarily at the civilian population the bombers caused heavy casualties. The first 1000-bomber raid by the RAF took place on 30 May 1942 against Cologne: 600 acres were destroyed and 45,000 people made homeless for the loss of 39 aircraft. The German blackout poster shows Death astride a British plane lobbing bombs at a lit-up target and warns: 'Black out! The enemy sees your light!' Bogner's biting sketch (*below*) concentrates on the barbarism of the bombing attacks as the girl asks the RAF officer: 'Darling, have you also been over Japan with your bombs?' He replies: 'No – why, do they have churches there too?' (Note the black barman.)

Royal Air Force . . .

Darling, bist du mit deinem Bomber auch schon mal über Japan gewesen?
No — wieso, gibt's dort auch alte Kirchen?
Bogner, *Das Schwarze Korps*,
16 July 1942

Das britische Einhorn

NORD-AFRIKA

Fernost

Zeichnung: Bogner

Verbohrt . . .

Bogner, *Das Schwarze Korps*, 12 March 1942

The war in the North African desert in which the Allies had had such success against Graziani's Italian troops took a distinct turn for the worse after the arrival of General Rommel and German forces in Tripoli in February 1941. For the next 18 months, fighting swept to and fro across the desert, with Rommel generally getting by far the better of it. This period of Allied setbacks is reflected in Bogner's cartoon (*left*). The British unicorn (a mythical creature) finds itself caught in the palm trees of North Africa, a coconut bomb falling to deliver the *coup de grâce*, while a sign points to the destruction of the Far East. All around the British tanks and planes lie broken and the one-word caption reads: 'Ridiculous.'

However, the boot was soon on the other foot. The decisive Second Battle of El Alamein (25 October-4 November), with General Bernard Montgomery now in charge of Eighth Army and the Germans' supply-line stretched to its limit, finally broke the back of the Afrika Korps. Harassed from the air and

'Tell that to the Marines'
H B Armstrong, *Melbourne Argus*, 1943

JAPS VICTORIOUS AT SOLOMONS

short of fuel and ammunition, the Axis armies were forced to retrace their steps back across the desert. Low's cartoon (*below*), with its reference to Edgar Allan Poe's poem *The Raven*, contrasts starkly with Bogner's of nine months earlier.

LUFTWAFFE

TO TRIPOLI TUNIS AND THE END OF THE AFRICAN LINE

ROMMEL

'Quoth the Eagle, "Nevermore"'
David Low, *Evening Standard*, 15 December 1942

At the outbreak of hostilities in the Pacific, the Japanese Fleet had a great superiority in aircraft carriers; they correctly believed that future naval battles would be won and lost with airborne weaponry. Luckily for the Allies, most of the US Navy's carriers had been on an exercise at sea at the time of Pearl Harbor and their successes in the naval battles of the Coral Sea and Midway Island quickly redressed the balance in the Pacific War.

The Coral Sea battle in May 1942 was a tactical success for the Allies, but the Japanese still held numerical superiority at sea. Thus, in an attempt to lure the remains of the United States' Pacific Fleet into an ambush, the Japanese next planned an invasion of the American base at Midway Island, Hawaii. However, United States codebreakers discovered the plan and the Americans caught the Japanese Fleet unawares. Four Japanese carriers and sundry other craft were destroyed by United States naval aircraft, making the battle a significant turning point in the Pacific War.

In the battle for the Solomon Islands, the Japanese again ran into difficulties. On the largest island of the group, Guadalcanal, they had begun to build an airfield but were overrun in August 1942 by US Marines. The territory was fiercely disputed in the following months and the opposing navies engaged in a series of battles for supremacy of the seas which left the American forces in command. However, Japanese radio announced the result as a complete victory over the United States as Roth's cartoon ironically points out. During this confrontation considerable success was achieved by US PT (torpedo) boats against Japanese shipping, as the drawing by Charles Addams (1912-88) – better known for his ghoulish 'Addams Family' series in the *New Yorker* – illustrates. (Lieut. John F Kennedy was commander of PT-109 in this theater, giving Addams' drawing a remarkably prophetic quality.)

'Did I ever tell you I was voted "Most Likely to Succeed" at Lafayette in 1938?'
Charles Addams, *New Yorker War Album*, London, 1943

'After heavy fighting we have established a very important base in the Pacific' – Tokyo radio
Stephen Roth, *Jesters in Earnest*, London, 1943

The rising sun at Midway
Daniel Fitzpatrick, *St Louis Post-Dispatch*, 16 July 1942

Gino Boccasile, Italian poster, c1942

G Bertoletti, Italian poster, 1943

'The Big Three will tie the enemy in knots'
Kukryniksi, Soviet poster, 1942

SPK, German poster for France, c1942

Posters were a commonly employed form of propaganda in World War II. Television was still in its infancy, film lacked instant impact and newspapers and magazines still suffered (in Europe at least) from wartime restrictions on color printing. However, no such problems arose for the government-sponsored poster campaigns, as these five examples bear witness. The picture of the octopus-limbed Churchill (*right*), his tentacles suitably lopped off at the sites of appropriate Axis victories, was produced for French consumption and reads: 'Have confidence . . . his amputations continue methodically.' The Kukryniksi group's Hitler poster (*below left*) shows the arms of the Big Three allies reaching out to tighten the stranglehold on the dictator himself now that his country lies in ruins. 'Ecco il Nemico' ('This is the enemy') is in fact an American poster for Italians, warning them of the dangers of fighting for Germany. It won its designers the 'Artist for Victory' competition in 1942. Bertoletti's 'Pax Britannica,' by contrast, was printed in Milan and shows a fat Jewish John Bull striding through the ruins, having swallowed the world. In Gino Boccasile's famous Italian poster (*top left*) depicting the cultural barbarism of the American troops, the black American sergeant, his features transformed nearly into a gorilla's face, grasps Greek art treasures, ludicrously underpriced, with animal savagery.

US poster, 1942

Mrs Laval, matchmaker
Adolf Hoffmeister, *Jesters in Earnest*, London, 1943

Threatened in the south by the Allied success at El Alamein and the landings under General Eisenhower in French North Africa (Operation Torch), German troops moved into unoccupied France on 11 November 1942, with the connivance of the French deputy premier Pierre Laval. Hoffmeister presents Laval as a procuress tempting Hitler with the naked Marianne (*left*). The American Fitzpatrick has Laval as a vulture perched on a gaunt swastika tree.

With the invasion of Vichy France by the Germans, the Allies were naturally concerned for the fate of the still substantial French Fleet at anchor in the Mediterranean port of Toulon. Separate negotiations by Eisenhower with the Vichy Admiral Darlan, offering him the post of head of the French government in North Africa, brought about the scuttling of the entire flotilla before the Germans could reach it. Darlan also eased the Torch landings in French-held Algeria through a command to stop Vichy resistance there. This deal between an American general and a Nazi collaborator caused considerable embarrassment in the Allied camp and outright hostility from General De Gaulle, Soviet ambassador Ivan Maisky and Roosevelt's envoy Wendell Willkie.

Stephen Roth's cartoon has Hitler rowed by Laval in a dinghy named the *Graf Spee* (the German battleship which had itself been scuttled in the early days of the war). However, Darlan was an embarrassment to the Allies once he had served his purpose. The matter was fortuitously resolved when the admiral was assassinated in Algiers on Christmas Eve, 1942.

Toulon, 1942
Stephen Roth, *Divided They Fall*, London, 1942

**'Frenchmen,
I bespeak the New Order'**
Daniel Fitzpatrick,
St Louis Post-Dispatch,
28 June 1942

General improvement in German morale
Boris Efimov, 1942

The Führer's barrel-organ
Boris Efimov, 1942

The enormous cost in German lives and equipment suffered in the campaigns on the Eastern Front caused Hitler and the German people great anxiety. After the success of the early years of the war, the losses in Russia and North Africa brought about a general depression in the population which Goebbels' propaganda ministry did its best to counter. Active measures were taken to put on a bright face and take an optimistic view, but the mood had changed. In Efimov's street-corner scene, civilians wearing jolly masks disguising their gloom do not fool Hitler, Himmler and Goebbels. In the foreground a man reads death announcements in the newspaper, while a mother holds her son's killed-in-action notice. The original subtitle read: 'Total eradication of pessimism and depression.' In the barrel-organ cartoon, subtitled 'Measures to cheer people up. No charge', axeman Himmler carries the message 'Look cheerful' on his blade and Goebbels parrots 'P . . . p . . . patience.'

Alan Schomburg, *Speed Comics* (cover), April 1943

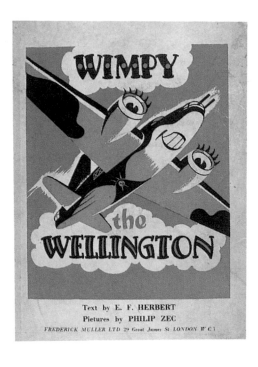

Next morning, Wimpy was wakened up by a tremendous noise, and when he opened his eyes, there were crowds of people still there, and, right in front of him, was a big black shiny car, and in the back of the car was sitting . . . who do you think ? . . . nobody else but THE PRESIDENT OF THE U.S.A. ! He had got up early and gone without his breakfast especially to come and see Wimpy and thank him for rescuing the Very Famous General.

So then the President made a little speech (which must have been *very* flattering, because Wimpy, who is really rather modest, would never tell me what he said, so I can't tell you, and you'll just have to make it up for yourself). And then some men came up with a big pot of GOLD PAINT.

And they painted a Huge Gold Bomb on Wimpy's nose and then the President himself signed it and Wimpy was so excited that he nearly made himself cross-eyed trying to squint at it !

E F Herbert, *Wimpy the Wellington*, London, 1942

Children's comics also reflected the war situation and for a short while *The Beano* ran a strip called 'Musso the Wop' portraying an incompetent dictator. Lord Snooty and his gang also tackled the enemy as did Superman, Captain Freedom and the various 'superheroes' of American magazines, as the cover of *Speed Comics* (*left*) illustrates.

Children's war interest was also catered for by the publication of humorous illustrated storybooks (*top*). 'Wimpy' was the RAF's nickname for the Vickers Wellington twin-engined bomber, which was probably the best of its type until the advent of the heavier, four-engined Avro Lancaster. The job of anthropomorphizing the plane, complete with waistcoat button and eyes in the engine nacelles, was done by the political cartoonist of the *Daily Mirror*, Philip Zec.

Frank Reynolds (1876-1953) contributed his first cartoon to *Punch* in 1906 and was art editor from 1920 to 1930. In *The Good-Tempered Pencil* (1956), Fougasse describes him as 'a latter-day John Leech with the added fluidity and linear "expression" that process [printing] allowed.' Here he portrays a supposedly typical German family.

One hundred per cent
Frank Reynolds, *Punch*, 19 October 1942

The arrival of American troops in Britain in January 1942 was not received with universal pleasure by the resident population, particularly those in the British armed forces who, on lower wages and severely hampered by military restrictions, felt that the Americans were 'overpaid, oversexed and over here.' However, their presence gave cartoonists plenty of good material for humor, as this selection from the pages of *Punch* bears witness.

Rowland Emett (1906-90) had his first cartoon published in *Punch* in 1939 while he was a draughtsman working on the development of the jet engine. His extraordinary cartoons – often showing his obsession for Victoriana, railways, tramcars and mechanical paraphernalia – have been much admired and have appeared in many advertising campaigns as well as such magazines as *Vogue*, *Life* and *Harper's Bazaar*.

'They say, can we do two hundred and eighty-seven Dainty Afternoon Teas?'
Rowland Emett, *Punch*, 2 February 1944

'They won't let on who the camp is for'
Acanthus, *Punch*, 16 December 1942

'Dear Momma, in England they drive on the left side of the road'
Anton, *Punch*, 8 April 1942

Right: This cartoon by the *Mirror*'s Philip Zec caused a furore when it was published in Britain. Indeed, it very nearly got the newspaper, which had one of the widest circulations in the war years, completely banned. The cartoon was interpreted as implying that the oil companies were making huge profits from fuel ferried at great risk by Britain's merchant seamen. Zec himself was later to explain that it was part of a series about the abuses of the system by black marketeers and an attack on the wastage of both food and fuel. The first cartoon had shown a black marketeer placing flowers on the tomb of a dead soldier saying: 'Poor fellow, now what can I sell his mother?' The second had emphasized the importance of not wasting food. This, the third in the series, was to make people aware that every drop of petrol was precious. By increasing the price of fuel the government had drawn attention to this fact, but to really hit home, Zec wanted to say that lives were being lost bringing tankers to Britain and that wastage was thus immoral. The original caption was 'Petrol is dearer now,' but with the new wording it soon appeared as a poster in petrol stations and big stores. The drawing was discussed heatedly in the House of Commons and Home Secretary Herbert Morrison believed it was a 'wicked cartoon.' The *Mirror* was eventually let off with a severe reprimand.

The price of petrol has been increased by one penny – Official
Philip Zec, *Daily Mirror*, 6 March 1942

Bert Thomas, British poster, 1942

Right: At a time when fuel was short and public transport was increasingly required for military purposes, the British government launched a campaign to discourage any civilian travel that was not absolutely necessary. This famous poster by Bert Thomas was produced by the Railway Executive Committee and was much in evidence from March 1942 onwards.

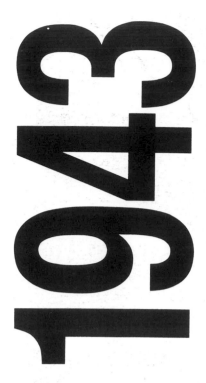

1943

By July 1943 all Axis forces had surrendered in North Africa, 300,000 had been killed or captured at Stalingrad, the Japanese had suffered further defeats in the Solomons and Sicily had fallen in another massive Allied counterattack in the Mediterranean. At the same time new Red Army assaults had begun to drive the Germans westwards across mainland Europe, while the strategic air offensive from Britain began concentrated 'area' bombing of major German cities in an attempt to break civilian morale, culminating in the incineration of Hamburg and (from November) the Battle of Berlin.

With the fall of Sicily, Mussolini had been forced to resign. When Allied troops landed on the Italian mainland in September, the Italian Army surrendered. Only rapid redeployment of its armies enabled Germany to defend the peninsula. On 23 September Mussolini, who had escaped from captivity, set up the Italian Socialist Republic in German-occupied Italy. Three weeks later the official Italian government declared war on the Nazis.

South East Asia Command (SEAC) was formed in August to coordinate the disparate forces fighting under Chinese, American and British Empire leadership, and fresh concerted attacks on the Japanese in the jungles of Burma – supported and supplied almost entirely by air – began to make significant inroads in that theatre as well.

For the Allies, so long the oppressed in the conflict thus far, the boot was now firmly on the other foot.

The first USAAF bomber raid on Italy took place in December 1942 and raids on Germany followed from late January 1943. The Eighth Air Force believed in a policy of precision bombing by daylight – in opposition to the RAF – using heavily armored B-17 'Flying Fortresses'. In attacks on Hamburg between 24 July and 3 August 1943, high-explosive and incendiary bombs dropped by 700 RAF and USAAF planes created a firestorm reaching 1000°C which destroyed over 6000 acres. About 50,000 civilians died and a million homeless fled the city. Similar concentrated attacks took place on other German cities, notably Berlin in 1944 and Dresden in 1945, with equally devastating results. The Axis response is clear: in 'Terror-flyers' by Fips, the 'Jewish conspiracy' lies behind the British bomb aimer's every action. 'Murder' is written across the sky. And in Boccasile's Italian poster (*opposite*) the American aviators are depicted as Chicago gangsters. The caption reads: 'The inhuman crimes of the "gangster pilots" exclude the United States from the civilized world.' A 'Flying Fortress' passes overhead.

Below: Decorating aircraft with pin-ups and cartoon characters developed to a high art in the war. TARFU is an acronym for Things are Really Fouled Up (stronger language versions are also common), a derivative of SNAFU (Situation Normal All Fouled Up), which gave rise to Warner Brothers' series of animated wartime films about Private Snafu.

Terrorflieger
Der Judenknechte Talmudtaten
Den abgrundtiefen Haß verraten,
Mit dem Alljuda hetzt und schürt,
Weil es sein nahes Ende spürt.

Fips, *Der Stürmer*, No 30, 1943

United States bomber nose-art cartoons, artist unknown, n.d.

Gino Boccasile, Italian poster, 1943

The Allies, under General Eisenhower, invaded Sicily (Operation Husky) on 10 July 1943, following a preliminary airborne assault the previous night. Supported by Allied navies and air forces, the attack succeeded and, after fierce fighting, the island was cleared of Axis troops by 17 August. The fall of Sicily led directly to the sacking of Mussolini by the Fascist Grand Council. By 8 September the Allies had landed on the mainland of Italy and the Italian Army had surrendered.

The cartoon (*left*) by the Canadian Russell Brockbank (1913-79), later art editor of *Punch*, shows the combined operations offensive, using air cover to act as an umbrella for amphibious troops and mechanized armor, with parachutists dropping behind the battlefront. The Lancaster and Fenwick drawings (*right*) give a British interpretation of the Italian perspective (the Four Hundred was a club in London much frequented by military personnel).

Mussolini was forced to resign on 25 July 1943, being replaced by Marshal Pietro Badoglio. Shortly afterwards he was arrested and confined to Gran Sasso in the Abruzzi Mountains. From there he was later rescued by a commando group led by Otto Skorzeny and set up as a puppet ruler of German-occupied Italy. The two drawings by the Kukryniksi group (*below right*) show the abject misery of a conquered Mussolini (note the bootprint on the seat of his trousers in the 1944 version).

Russell Brockbank, *Lilliput*, December 1943

'Thank-a da Goodness I am no longer da General – now once-a more just-a your old friend Tonetti from-a da "Four Hundred" yes?'
Ian Fenwick, *Enter Trubshaw*, London, 1944

Osbert Lancaster, *Daily Express*, 12 July 1943

Kukryniksi, 1943

Mussolini
Kukryniksi, 1944

Nicolai Jiscenko, *Unter dem Zeichen des Hakenkreuzes*, unpublished sketchbook

These remarkable drawings were given to the senior UN Relief and Rehabilitation Administration officer in Hamburg by a woman in a transit camp for displaced persons in July 1945. The British officer, James Livesey, subsequently visited the dying artist in the camp and promised to bring the drawings to Britain, where they were eventually bequeathed to the Imperial War Museum. Livesey never saw the artist again but later learnt of Jiscenko's death in another camp, where he claimed to be Yugoslavian, though it is now believed that he was almost certainly Ukrainian. The drawings, 50 in all (of which, sadly, only 10 are finished), form a series about the Nazi years, *Beneath the Sign of the Swastika*, and include sections on Aryans, education, Hitler's 10th anniversary in power, and so on. Special speeches were made in Berlin on 30 January 1943 by Goebbels and Goering to celebrate the 10th anniversary. (The RAF also marked the occasion by interrupting the festivities with the first-ever daylight raid on the capital, using a group of Mosquito bombers whose arrival had been carefully timed.)

Three of the illustrations are reproduced here for the first time. The translations of the Hitler quotations have unfortunately not been made by a native English speaker, but the intention is clear. (*Vorwärts* is German for 'forward.')

Nightalarm...

Saul Steinberg, *PM*, 1943

With Italy's declaration of war on Germany on 13 October, Soviet successes in Eastern Europe and American progress in the Pacific War, a mood of confidence began to spread among the Allies. In Steinberg's *PM* cartoon of Hitler as a chicken (*left*), the German armed forces wait in vain for the delivery of Victory while in his stomach, occupied by the countries swallowed whole by the Nazis, the fizzing bomb indicates an imminent explosion. (*Ersatz*, meaning 'substitute,' was commonly applied to the imitation goods produced when food was in short supply, for example, *Ersatzkaffee* for coffee made from acorns.) Pelc has the Big Three relaxing over the conference table (*top right*), Stalin smoking a Hitler pipe, Churchill using Mussolini's mouth as an ashtray and Roosevelt resting his head on a Tojo-rug. The cartoon by 'Bunbury' (the name, from Oscar Wilde's *The Importance of Being Earnest*, used by Osbert Lancaster for political drawings other than his pocket cartoons) harks back to the story of Belshazzar's feast in the Bible, in which the conqueror reads the writing on the wall indicating that his time is up. Also present are Goering, Goebbels, Ribbentrop, Himmler and, serving, Laval. Kem's Christmas card for 1943 (*below right*) has the Big Three chasing Hitler as a turkey ready to cook for their Yuletide feast.

'Don't give it a thought, boss – it's just an old Jewish gag'
Bunbury, *Sunday Express*, 1943

Victory Club
A Pelc, *Jesters in Earnest*, London, 1943

Kem, Christmas card, December 1943

JANE ...

The hugely popular pin-up character, Jane, who gave a new meaning to the phrase 'strip cartoon,' started life very modestly as a Bright Young Thing who always got into scrapes in a series called 'Jane's Journal' drawn by Norman Pett. However, her star ascended in December 1938 when Don Freeman began writing the storyline at the *Mirror* management's behest and introduced the idea of playfully shedding items of her clothing during her adventures. When war broke out she met up with a handsome Secret Service officer called Georgie Porgie with whom she fell in love. Accompanied by her faithful dachshund, Fritz, Jane later traveled to France with the NAAFI, to be near Georgie, who had gone over for the Normandy landings. (Mike Hubbard took over the drawing in 1948 until its final episode on 10 October 1959.)

Jane had tremendous appeal among the Allied forces and when she appeared totally naked once, the United States service paper of the Far East, *Round-Up*, commented: 'Jane peeled a week ago. The British 36th Division immediately gained six miles and the British attacked in the Arakan. Maybe we Americans ought to have Jane, too!' The great Fleet Street figure, Hannen Swaffer, talking of Jane's influence on the RAF in 1943, commented: 'The morale of the RAF depended on how much clothing she had left off in the *Daily Mirror* that morning. A legend grew up that Jane always stripped for victory. She was the anti-Gremlin.'

'I'm afraid we shall have to leave building the new wing until after the war'
Rowland Emett, *Punch*, 17 March 1943

With the introduction of the British Lancaster bomber, the new Mustang long-range escort fighter and the remarkable De Havilland Mosquito twin-engined fighter-bomber, Allied aircraft were very much in the public eye in 1943 – particularly after the successes of Bomber Command over Germany. It is thus not surprising that they featured increasingly in one-off jokes in the cartoon pages of the newspapers at the time. Joe Lee in the *Evening News* shows war artists painting from the wing of a Lancaster, while Emett has a bomber thundering overhead in a quiet rural scene.

'First it was war reporters. Now it's official artists'
Joe Lee, *Evening News*, 22 January 1943

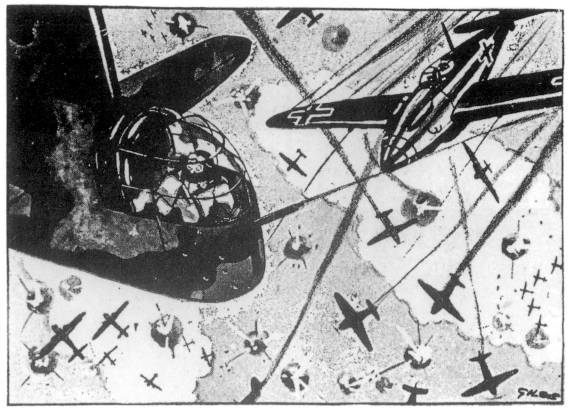

'Dear Mum. I'm sorry to hear Willie's got measles and that Uncle George fell down stairs but didn't hurt himself much . . .'

Carl Giles, *Reynolds News*, 18 February 1940

'For the last time, Madam, this is not the Baby Linen Counter'

Carl Giles, *Reynolds News*, 17 March 1940

Formerly an animator for Alexander Korda's studios, Carl Giles (1916-95) became a regular contributor to the Sunday newspaper *Reynolds News* from 1937 to 1943, when he moved to join Express Newspapers, drawing for the *Sunday Express* and later for the *Daily Express* as well. In 1944 he was sent to the front as the first ever official cartoonist war correspondent and provided many fascinating reports, both verbal and pictorial, from the battlezone.

Giles' sense of the absurd is admirably displayed in these cartoons from the early days of the war: the tail-gunner's nonchalant letter-writing when all around him the sky is ablaze with enemy fighters; the crossed line on the field telephone; the ludicrous picnicker gag - all make us laugh despite ourselves. The 'Young Ernie' strip Wa8 a captionless three-frame cartoon that ran in parallel with his topical drawings in *Reynolds News*. (This version has been adapted for Dutch consumption.)

Young Ernie
Carl Giles, *Reynolds News*, 12 November 1939

'All right, all right. You carry on. You'll soon find out WHY it's silly to sit there'
Carl Giles, *Reynolds News*, 26 January 1941

'What a life! I haven't even got a chance to commit hara-kiri!'

Stephen Roth, *Divided They Fall*, London, 1943

**'The Columbia Broadcasting System interrupts this program
to bring you a special news bulletin . . .'**

Peter Arno, *New Yorker War Album*, London, 1943

Left: With the completion of the Guadalcanal campaign in February 1943, the next major event of the Pacific war was the Battle of the Bismarck Sea off the north coast of New Guinea, in March. A Japanese troop convoy lost all eight transport ships and four destroyers to Australian and American airmen supported by torpedo boats. A number of naval actions also accompanied the island-hopping advance of MacArthur's forces through Melanesia and Micronesia toward the mainland of Japan itself. The assault on the Marianas group on 15 June 1944 was hotly contested by the Japanese Fleet in what became known as the Battle of the Philippine Sea. However, the Japanese attack was fended off with such great success (over 240 planes and two carriers destroyed for minimal loss) that it was described by American servicemen as the 'Great Marianas Turkey Shoot.' In October United States landings on Leyte in the Philippines led to a huge naval conflict, the Battle of Leyte Gulf. The Japanese lost three battleships, 10 heavy cruisers, four aircraft carriers and numerous destroyers and smaller ships, again for relatively little damage to the American forces. It was indeed a depressing time for the Japanese, as these two cartoons illustrate.

Right: As the war progressed, domestic travel was severely limited. All forms of petroleum, from motor spirit to engine oil, were strictly rationed and military requirements took precedence. Knock, witty as ever in the third issue of the German propaganda broadsheet, *Vox*, makes high comedy out of an official announcement from the White House that Eleanor Roosevelt would shop for herself and the President by bicycle to save fuel. (*Vox*, dropped by air, lampooned selected items in Allied newspapers published during the week and illustrated the stories with its own cartoons.)

Sonntag

Frau Roosevelt gab bekannt, daß sie in Zukunft, um Benzin für Verteidigungszwecke zu sparen, ihre Einkäufe auf dem Fahrrad erledigen wird.

Dimanche

Madame Roosevelt annonce que désormais elle fera ses emplettes à bicyclette, afin d'économiser l'essence pour des buts de défense nationale.

Sunday

Frau Roosevelt recently announced that she would henceforward do her shopping on a bicycle, in order that the benzine go for defence purposes.

Wir bringen hier ein Bild ihrer ersten benzinlosen Einkaufsfahrt.

Et la voici après une visite au marché!

Here is an illustration of her first benzin-less shopping expedition.

Knock, *Vox*, No 3, 1941

H Groth and L Kade, *So wird man Fallschirmjäger*, Berlin, 1943

Fougasse, RAF training poster, 1942

Cartoons were much used in training manuals and the like by both sides during World War II. The figure of Pilot Officer Prune (*below right*) is a familiar one to anyone who was taught the rudiments of aviation through the monthly issues of *Tee Emm* – short for Training Memorandum. Drawn by Bill Hooper ('Raff'), such was the character's success – and that of his colleagues, including AC2 Plonk – that a number of books, with text by *Punch* writer Anthony Armstrong, followed, under titles such as *Nice Types, Goodbye Nice Types* and *Plonk's Party*. The portrait of Prune shown here was reproduced in a line-only variant in *Tee Emm* for January 1943.

Fougasse, as well as drawing his 'Careless Talk Costs Lives' posters for the Ministry of Information, also created a series of instructional drawings for the Air Ministry, an example of which is given here (*below left*). The Germans also used cartoons as a teaching aid, as can be seen from the two illustrations (*above left*) by Hermann Groth for a book, *So you Want to be a Paratrooper*, with rhyming verse by Ludwig Kade. The last drawing of the book has Churchill being pursued by a (now fully trained) *Fallschirmjäger*.

The word 'gremlin' originated as RAF slang in 1941. The Oxford English Dictionary is unable to explain its derivation, except perhaps by some comparison to the word 'goblin,' but defines a gremlin as: 'A mischievous sprite imagined as the cause of mishaps to aircraft.' Hurriedly produced from factories and rapidly returned to the air by ground crew after battle sorties that often defied the manufacturer's specifications on endurance, speed and ceiling, it is not surprising that there were frequent malfunctions in aircraft on both sides during the war. Conversely, with planes limping home on one engine with control wires shot away and gaping holes in place of lifting surfaces – as frequently happened – the wonder is nobody invented a mythical creature (other than 'guardian angel') to describe the opposite influence (though see 'Jane' on p. 106). The children's book by Marshall and Royce (*top right*) was illustrated by Len Kirley.

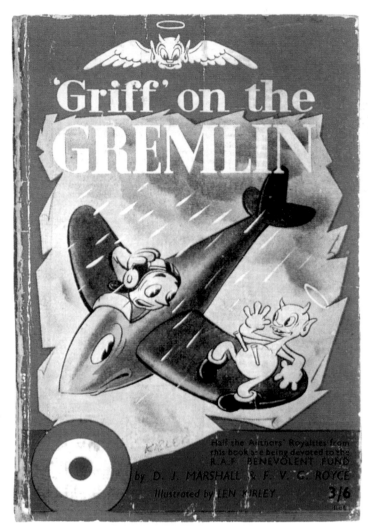

D J Marshall and F V G Royce, *Griff on the Gremlin*, London, 1943

P/O Prune says, 'A good landing is one you can walk away from'
Raff, 1943

Le chef Darnand: 'Eh! bien, que dites-vous de mon serment milicien?'
J Sennep, 1943

Three views of Vichy France. Joseph Darnand was an enthusiastic supporter of the Nazi regime and in January 1943 organized a Gestapo-style French military police force, known as the Milice Française, for the brutal suppression of the French Resistance and their sympathizers. In the above cartoon by Jean Pennes (b. 1894), who drew under the name 'Jehan Sennep,' Milice troops resemble swastikas as they kneel to swear allegiance. The caption reads: 'Well, what do you think of my Milice oath?'

Graffiti was perhaps the safest form of passive resistance to the Nazis and walls were often scrawled with the Allied 'V for Victory' sign or its Morse Code equivalent. Such was Pétain's unpopularity in Vichy France, however, that Sennep depicts the marshal furtively writing slogans in support of his own regime (*below*).

Propagande
J Sennep, 1943

France today
Arthur Szyk, *The New Order*, New York, 1940

Two more views of Nazi occupation. The evil-looking Hitlerite mosquito sucking blood in the Middle East (*right*) has much similarity with Efimov's picture of the Nazi cockroaches with their heads in the trough of Europe. (The labels read: 'Dutch cheese,' 'French wine,' 'Norwegian fish,' 'Rumanian maize,' 'Hungarian wheat,' 'Italian macaroni,' 'Greek olives.')

Occupation allemande
Stanislaw Dobrzynski, *Sein Kampf*, Jerusalem, 1944

The 'New Order' organization of the economy of Europe
Boris Efimov, 1942

H M Bateman, British poster, c1942

De Vampyr
L J Jordaan, *Der Groene Amsterdammer*, 1940

Posters alerting the population about health hazards and food shortages were common during wartime. The cartoon (*left*) by Australian-born artist H M Bateman (1887-1970) – best known for his 'the Man who . . .' drawings of the 1920s and 1930s – is one of a series of eight he produced for the British Ministry of Health. The 'Squander Bug' (originally the 'Money Grub') was designed by Phillip Boydell to encourage people to buy savings stamps rather than squander what little money they had on unnecessary goods. The 'pot luck' poster also has a clear message.

Phillip Boydell, British poster, 1942

British poster, c1942

Left: Another view of Europe's economy as arranged under the Nazi 'New Order' policy. Jordaan's powerful vampire image has Germany sucking the very lifeblood out of Holland (note the gasmask and bayonet-blade spinal fins).

The six cartoons reproduced on this page were designed by Kem in imitation of an episode in an illuminated version of the Persian national epic, the *Shanamah* or Book of Kings. Originally printed as postcards, the sequence reads from left to right as follows: (1) 'On Zohhak's shoulders by magic two serpents grew, and destruction came forth from that man'; (2) 'Secret became the law of wise men, and the desires of mad men became disseminated. The hand of administration became long for an evil purpose, goodness found no graceful expression'; (3) 'Thus he saw that from the palace of the Emperor, three warriors suddenly came forward . . .'; (4) 'He cried and raised his hand before the Shah: "My Shah, I am Kava asking for justice. There must be an end to oppression and there must be at least a pretext for oppression"'; (5, *enlarged picture right*) 'Strongly he secured his two hands and waist, so that his fetters could not be broken even by a fierce elephant'; (6) 'Swift as a racer, he brought Zohhak away, and put him into confinement on the mountain of Damavend, and when the name of Zohhak became earth, the world was wholly cleansed of his evil.'

In the enlarged detail Churchill (note white charger), Roosevelt and Stalin accompany Hitler with 'magic serpents' Tojo and Mussolini whilst Goebbels is dragged behind by the horse's tail.

بندی ببستش دو دست و میان

که نگشاید آن بندپیل ژیان

Kem, postcards for Middle East, c1943

117

1944

In Europe 1944 was the decisive year of the war. On the Eastern Front, Soviet forces lifted the siege of Leningrad in January, and this success was followed by a series of massive offensives that took the Red Army through the Ukraine and Belorussia into Poland, Hungary and Rumania.

In the West, the long-awaited Second Front was at last opened with the Normandy landings in June. Further landings followed in the south of France in August. Breaking out from Normandy, Allied forces swept across northern France and Belgium, liberating Paris and Brussels by early September. An attempt on Hitler's life by disaffected generals added further stress in the Nazi camp. It seemed that the war might be over before the end of the year.

But German resistance stiffened both in the East and the West. In December the Wehrmacht was even able to launch a last-ditch counteroffensive in the Ardennes – the Battle of the Bulge. The overwhelming power of the Allied forces, however, proved decisive against a by now poorly equipped German Army. The final defeat of Germany was clearly only a matter of time.

In the Pacific, the Japanese were being slowly driven back, although they put up desperate resistance. The Battle of Leyte Gulf off the Philippines in October effectively destroyed what remained of the Japanese Fleet, despite fierce suicide attacks by aircraft and ships. By the end of the year, in this theater too an ultimate Allied victory appeared inevitable, but much hard fighting still lay ahead.

Optimisme ved nytaaret, 1943-44

Harald Engman, 1943-44

This is one of a number of Scandinavian resistance cartoons later collected in the book *Den Forbudte Maler* (1945). It was drawn by the Danish artist, Harald Engman, and shows a fresh-faced soldier parachuting from a free Denmark on to German soil, holding a tank with 'Churchill' and 'Freedom' written on it. The heavily defeated German Army hobbles off into a cave labelled 'To the history department,' leaving only corpses and a couple of soldiers behind. Notice the fizzing bomb about to destroy these last remnants. The caption reads: 'Optimistic New Year, 1943-44.'

After the Italian surrender in September 1943 the Germans poured troops into the peninsula and defended the Gustav Line to the south of Rome, centred on Monte Cassino. In an attempt to outflank this formidable position, the Allies launched a seaborne assault 60 miles further up the coast at Anzio on 22 January 1944. But the 50,000 troops, mostly American servicemen of VI Corps under Major-General John Lucas, soon found themselves under heavy counterattack from German troops and decided to dig in. The lot of the GI on the Anzio beaches is portrayed with feeling by one of their number, Bill Mauldin (1921-2003) – later to win a Pulitzer Prize. These two drawings (*right*) feature his famous bedraggled duo, Willie and Joe.

'Forever, Amen. Hit the dirt!'
Bill Mauldin, *Stars and Stripes*, 1944

**'I can't get no lower, Willie.
Me buttons is in th'way'**
Bill Mauldin, *Stars and Stripes*, 1944

While the world's attention was often focussed elsewhere, General Slim's Fourteenth Army, which came to be described as the 'Forgotten Army', had begun to hit back in Burma. After arduous training, a long-range penetration force known as the Chindits (after a Burmese mythical beast, the Chinthe) were among the first to take the war to the Japanese. By January 1945 half of Burma was in Allied hands. The illustration (*left*) by John Musgrave-Wood (1915-99) later known as 'Emmwood,' shows the unpleasant reality of jungle warfare. The diminutive Gurkhas who fought with the British Empire troops were much respected allies as Musgrave-Wood, himself a Chindit, illustrates (*below*).

**'When this is all over I suppose some ape will
write a book about it and try to make out it was funny'**
P Boyle and J Musgrave-Wood,
Jungle, Jungle,
Little Chindit, London, 1944

**Gurkhas – Lilliputian men
with a capacity for winning
VCs in all theatres of war**
P Boyle and J Musgrave-Wood,
Jungle, Jungle,
Little Chindit, London, 1944

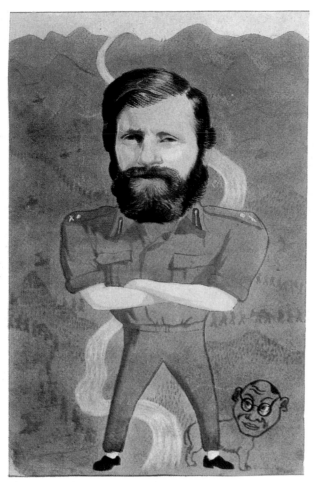

Major General Orde Wingate
Ghansi, 23 December 1943

Left: The leader of the Chindits was the charismatic Orde Wingate. He is shown here in a portrait by Ghansi astride the Burma Road essential for Allied support of the Chinese leader, Chiang Kai-shek. Wingate was killed in an air crash in March 1944.

German aerial leaflet, c1944

After the initial breakthrough in Italy, the Allied forces dug in opposite the Gothic Line as the Soviets rolled up former Nazi-occupied territories in the East. During this period Hitler could ill afford yet another offensive from the immediate south and thus leaflets like 'Meet Charlie the Gunner' were dropped on Allied troops stationed in Italy. Unfortunately for Hitler, they did not have the required effect. The British Eighth Army and US Fifth Army broke through in April 1945.

Russell Brockbank's depiction of life on the Italian Front (*opposite*) is closer to the actual situation than the Axis powers would have liked to believe.

'I suppose you realize you're driving on the wrong side of the road'
Russell Brockbank, *Punch*, 22 July 1944

'You won't half cop it for being late for the invasion'
Acanthus, *Punch*, 2 August 1944

The Allies invaded Normandy on 6 June 1944 (Operation Overlord) at beaches between Quinéville and Ouistreham, having successfully duped the Germans into believing that the attack would come further east on the coastline of the Pas de Calais. The five-pronged force of four army corps and three airborne divisions established beachheads codenamed Utah, Omaha, Gold, Juno and Sword. Some 150,000 men landed on the first day, supported by 6000 assorted ships and over 12,000 planes of various kinds. The invasion was a complete success and, despite determined counterattacks by the Germans, the Allies had reached the Seine by the autumn. On 15 August they launched a second assault in southern France, codenamed Operation Anvil/Dragoon, to begin a pincer action.

Stephen Roth's 'Sword of Damocles' cartoon (*left*) alludes to Dionysius I, tyrant of ancient Syracuse, who invited Damocles to dine with him, a sword suspended by a hair above the guest's head. This story, illustrating the tyrant's life of luxury at the cost of insecurity, is very appositely used by Roth. Hitler's anxiety is evident as Churchill counts down to D-Day and the start of the 'Second Front' invasion from the West. When the assault starts, Harald Engman, drawing in occupied Denmark, turns Churchill's cigar into an enormous cannon – 'A strong cigar' – as the Axis powers, with Mussolini on crutches and Tojo barefooted, retreat (*above right*). The defenseworks show Germany's last three barriers: the Adolf Hitler Line, the Gothic Line and the Siegfried Line, behind which are ranged antique cannon. Bill Crawford (b. 1913) has Hitler at bayonet point holding grimly on to a crumbling swastika (*below right*), while the Acanthus joke (*above*) harks back to Dunkirk, when the bravery of so many small boat owners helped rescue the retreating Allies.

The Sword of Damocles
Stephen Roth, *Divided They Fall*, London, 1943

En staerk cigar
Harald Engman, 1944

This is it!
Bill Crawford, *Newark Evening News*, 1944

'Wait for it, wait for it'
Russell Brockbank, *Punch*, 4 April 1945

On 17 September 1944, three Allied airborne divisions were dropped into Belgium and the Netherlands with the aim of capturing the main river and canal bridges for the advancing ground troops. The operation, codenamed Market Garden, was generally successful, except for the fifth bridge, over the Rhine at Arnhem, where the British and Polish parachutists landed too far from the objective and were overwhelmed by superior German numbers. Of a force of 10,000, over half were captured and more than 1000 killed.

Russell Brockbank's drawing illustrates an episode that actually took place. The over-eager driver was, of course, killed but miraculously the glider pilot survived to tell the tale. The magnificent illustration by Jordaan (*opposite*), 'The Last Round,' has Hitler, Goebbels and Goering as three of the apocalyptic horsemen speeding past a burning Dutch townscape (after a picture by Böcklin whose *Toteninsel* was so admired by the Nazis). The German view of all this 'liberation' is heavily emphasized in a poster for Holland (*below left*) alluding to the degeneracy of the United States: negroes jitterbugging, Judaism everywhere, even Betty Grable's million-dollar leg can be seen as the Liberation monster bombs the Low Countries.

German poster for Holland, 1944

De laaste ronde
J Jordaan, *Der Groene Amsterdammer*, 1944

Crack
David Low, *Evening Standard*, 24 July 1944

Vicky, *News Chronicle*

The bomb plot to assassinate Adolf Hitler at his headquarters in Rastenburg, East Prussia, on 20 July 1944 implicated a great many generals Hitler had hitherto felt able to trust, and added to the paranoia he was suffering. Now alking with a limp and with an injured arm and cut ear, Hitler began a major purge. Von Stauffenberg, who planted the bomb, was shot the following day and the leading conspirators were quickly rounded up and hanged from meat-hooks to die a slow and grisly death. Hitler himself now took over the conduct of the war. As Low's cartoon indicates, Himmler was put in charge of the purge. Giles (*below*) has a diminutive Hitler hiding behind the Gestapo chief's legs.

'I alone decide the policy of Germany'
Carl Giles, *Daily Express*, 25 July 1944

On the Eastern Front, meanwhile, the German situation was bleak. Stalingrad was followed by the retreat from Leningrad (*left*) and defeat in the great tank battle of Kursk. By the end of 1943 the Nazis had been driven back to Kiev on the Dniepr – the *Ostwall* or fortified 'Winter Line' which they had crossed with such high hopes two years before. Nine months later, with supplies running short and his former allies collapsing around him, Hitler's position was becoming desperate, as the two Low cartoons on this page show.

House of Cards
David Low, *Evening Standard*, 25 August 1944

'Will you take my IOU?'
David Low, *Evening Standard*, 22 September 1944

Ronald Searle, unpublished POW Christmas card, Changi, 1944

Cartoons helped enliven the dull routines of life in POW camps during the war. Perhaps the most celebrated cartoonist prisoner was Ronald Searle (b. 1920). He had begun contributing cartoons to local Cambridge newspapers when he was a teenager and had graduated to *Lilliput* and *Punch* when war broke out. Captured in Singapore in 1942, Searle spent the remaining years of the war as a prisoner of the Japanese.

His haunting sketches of life as a POW were published in the 1980s, but this cartoon Christmas card – one of a hand-drawn set produced for his fellow prisoners – shows a lighter side and is reproduced here for the first time.

Milos Zubac (b. 1922) was a POW in Stalag 344 at Lamsdorf in Germany from January 1944 to February 1945 where, though Yugoslavian, he somehow managed to have himself registered as a member of the Canadian Army and was hence interned with British and American servicemen. A series of his cartoons was presented to Britain's Imperial War Museum in 1987, following a brief visit by the artist. One of these is reproduced here, again for the first time. The series of comic illustrations of life in Lamsdorf camp includes pictures of a rugby match and, here, of a mess-tin meal prepared using an improvised hand-made bellows known as a 'blower.'

Bodo Gerstenberg, by contrast, was a German interned by the Americans in the POW camp at Fort Devens, where he produced illustrations for the fortnightly anti-Fascist POW magazine *PW*. A splendid cover drawing for the magazine, entitled 'Germany's gravediggers,' is reproduced here. The gravediggers are an SS officer and a Great War veteran.

Bodo Gerstenberg, *PW*, March 1945

The blower
Milos Zubac, POW drawing, Lamsdorf, Germany, 1944

With threats from the west and east, Germany had occupied Hungary on 19 March 1944 in an effort to check the Soviet advance. But by August the Russians had overrun Rumania and the Crimea, and they moved into Bulgaria in September. Finland ceased hostilities against the Soviet Union on 4 September. Th Th Heine (1867-1948) was one of the founder-members of *Simplicissimus* and produced over 2000 drawings for the magazine before, as a Jew, he was forced to leave, settling eventually in Sweden in 1942. The caption for his cartoon, 'The lyrical time of year,' runs as follows: 'Take note, Herr Horthy, we are a poetic nation. Whenever the first little flowers begin to bloom and the little birds start to sing, then spring fever moves our hearts and we feel a longing to begin a new bloody occupation!' (Admiral Miklos Horthy was Regent of Hungary from 1920 to 1944. When in October 1944 he expressed a desire to end Hungary's involvement in the war, his son was kidnapped by the Nazis and he was forced to abdicate.)

Die lyrische Jahreszeit
'Merken Sie sich, Herr Horthy, wir sind ein Volk der Dichter. Immer, wenn die ersten Blümelein sprießen und die Vöglein wieder zu zwitschern beginnen, dann bewegen Frühlingsgefühle unser Herz und erfüllen es mit Sehnsucht nach einer neuen blutigen Okkupation!'
Th Th Heine, 1944

'Military idiots with junk from the decadent democracies, to see the Führer'
Vicky, *Drawn by Vicky* (cover), London, 1944

Moi, je les aurais arrêtes à Verdun
Jean Effel, 1944

Paris was liberated on 25 August and by 11 September the Normandy and southern France invasion forces of the Allies had met up near Dijon. In the drawing (*left*) by 'Jean Effel' (b. 1908, real name François Lejeune), Pétain, in a cruel irony, is seen suggesting Verdun as the point where he would stop the advance (as he had done against the Germans in the Great War.

On 2 October 1944 the US First Army began an assault on the Siegfried Line, or Westwall, near Aachen. As the Nazis had bypassed the Maginot Line by outflanking it through the Low Countries, so the Allies quickly pressed home their attack in the weakest link of the enemy fortifications from the identical vantage point. Vicky's cover (*above*) for a collection of his drawings published in 1944 has Commander-in-Chief Eisenhower and Montgomery, leaders of the Allied armies in the West, knocking on the door of the Third Reich.

Boris Efimov, Soviet poster, 1941

Opposite top: Another 'reality versus illusion' portrait of Hitler, this time by Deni (1893-1946), real name Viktor Nikolaevich Denisov, who was a regular contributor to *Pravda* from 1921. The gruesome bloody portraits of Hitler and Himmler (*opposite below*) are by the Kukryniksi group.

Two Soviet attacks on the 'pure Aryan' ideal as applied to the Nazi leaders themselves. Boris Efimov (*above*) portrays Goebbels as a screaming Mickey Mouse with a swastika tail while the Kukryniksi group have Goebbels painting a fantasy Hitler from a decrepit original (*right*).

Kukryniksi, n.d.

Fascism equals conquering peace and serfdom for the people. The Red Army equals an amendment to the situation
Deni, Soviet poster, 1943

Hitler
Kukryniksi, 1944

Himmler
Kukryniksi, 1944

The Allies had been anxious for some time about what appeared to be man-made ski slopes on the Baltic coastline at Peenemünde. They proved to be launch-ramps for Hitler's latest secret weapon: the V1 cruise missile. Experiments had been made with pilotless planes and glider bombs earlier in the war, but the impact of the 'doodlebugs' or 'buzz-bombs', as they came to be called by their victims in London and the southern counties of England, was awesome. After their first appearance in June 1944, a number of measures were taken to defeat the new menace: bombing the launch-sites; tipping the wings by flying alongside them; and jamming the guidance system so that they fell short; but the final death-knell was sounded when anti-aircraft guns were brought down to the coast and they were destroyed in the air.

After the V1 came the V2, a larger and even more destructive rocket which fell soundlessly with massive impact and was not countered until the launch-sites were physically overrun by the advancing Allies. Pouwels' cartoon (*right*) of the amazed Churchill and British Lion (note Jewish and Communist symbols on the drapes and crystal ball) was published two months before the first V2 fell on Chiswick on 8 September.

De ziener van Downing-Street 10
Pouwels, *Storm SS*, 25 July 1944

Emett's mad inventor (*below*) has produced what looks like an aerial cannon which is not as far from reality for a V5 as might be thought – the projected V3 weapon was an enormous gun capable of lobbing shells from the Continent into the heart of London.

'Congratulations, Herr Professor! Our Fuehrer will now think up something for it to do'
Rowland Emett, *Punch*, 16 August 1944

Right and below: A remarkable spoof on Lewis Carroll's *Alice in Wonderland* with pastiche Tenniel illustrations by the *Punch* artist Norman Mansbridge. In the sample pages, Hitler is Alice, Chamberlain is the caterpillar and Heinrich Himmler (head of the SS) is the Queen of Hearts.

ADOLF IN BLUNDERLAND

JAMES DYRENFORTH & MAX KESTER
Illustrated by NORMAN MANSBRIDGE

James Dyrenforth and Max Kester,
Adolf in Blunderland, London, 1939

ADOLF IN BLUNDERLAND

EVERYONE. Heil !

ADOLF. (*Having the last word as usual.*) Heil !

QUEEN. What's your name, child ?

ADOLF. My name is Adolf, so please your Heartlessness.

QUEEN. And who are these three men lying on their faces ?

KING. They look to *me*, my dear, like some Storm Troopers after the storm.

(*There is a sycophantic titter.*)

QUEEN. *Silence !* Turn them over, Adolf—with your foot.

ADOLF. I'll do no such thing. Soldiers are sacred—except Generals.

QUEEN. Off with his Swastika !

KING. Consider, my dear : he is only a mental infant.

QUEEN. Get up, you there ! Now then, what have you been doing here ?

TWO. May it please your Heartlessness, we were trying—

QUEEN. In Germany, I and my Gestapo do the trying. You are guilty of subversive activities. Off with their Swastikas !

(*There is a commotion as her orders are ruthlessly carried out.*)

QUEEN. There ! That's good. And after dinner I'll go round and subdue them myself. That will make me feel better. Do you play anything ?

ADOLF. Who, me ?

QUEEN. Yes, little boy, you !

ADOLF. Well, if I had a piano, I could play " The Merry Widow " Waltz.

40

133

The Red Death
Adolf Hoffmeister, *Jesters in Earnest*, London, 1943

By the end of 1944 the German Army was in full retreat on all fronts. In Hoffmeister's drawing above, 'The Red Death' follows the German soldiers, retreating on foot and pillaging as they go, their eyes constantly set on the Red Army behind them. Sennep, meanwhile, shows us all the German generals eager for an armistice (*right*). As the carriage from Compiègne fills, Goering shouts: 'Hurry up, mein Führer, or you'll have to sign in the corridor.'

LE WAGON DE L'ARMISTICE

Le wagon de l'Armistice
'Dépêchez-vous, mon Führer, sans ça, vous risquez de signer dans le couloir!'
J Sennep, 1944

LA TRISTE HISTOIRE DE WINSTON CHURCHILL
descendant de John Churchill, duc de Marlborough

à la façon des Images d'Epinal.

Pour servir à l'édification des jeunes Français

Malbrough allait en guerre
Mironton, tonton, mirontaine !
Malbrough faisait la guerre:
C'était à Malplaquet. (ter)

En mil neuf cent quarante,
Mironton, tonton, mirontaine,
Son descendant déchante,
Il est mal embarqué ! (ter)

Sur les côtes de Norvège,
Mironton, tonton, mirontaine,
Churchill prend un bain d'siège
Et rembarque illico ! (ter)

Avec la peau des autres,
Mironton, tonton, mirontaine,
Avec la peau des autres,
L'Anglais est un héros ! (ter)

Il montre son adresse,
Mironton, tonton, mirontaine,
Pour les r'cords de vitesse,
L'Anglais est un champion..t

Faut voir comme il rembarque,
Mironton, tonton, mirontaine,
Faut voir comme il rembarque,
C'est sa spécialité ! (ter)

Sur mer est sa maîtrise,
Mironton, tonton, mirontaine,
J'allais dire traîtrise...
Le mot m'a z'échappé ! (ter)

Notre foudre de guerre,
Mironton, tonton, mirontaine,
Cherche un nouveau compère,
Pour le faire écharper. (ter)

Encore un plan superbe !
Mironton, tonton, mirontaine,
Allons derrièr' les Serbes,
Pour plus d'sécurité. (ter)

Débarquons à Athènes,
Mironton, tonton, mirontaine,
On pourra sans trop d'peine,
Après, se rembarquer ! (ter)

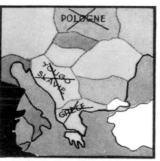

Faudra qu'tout l'monde y passe,
Mironton, tonton, mirontaine,
Quand un allié trépasse,
C'est la fatalité ! (ter)

Ne changeons pas d'tactique,
Mironton, tonton, mirontaine,
Même en Cyrénaïque,
Avançons à r'culons ! (ter)

J'mettrai l'feu à la Terre,
Mironton, tonton, mirontaine,
On verra qu'l'Angleterre
Peut encor décamper ! (ter)

A Malplaquet, grand-père,
A vaincu, mironton mirontaine,
Nos alliés, en cett' guerre,
Moi, j'les ai bien plaqués ! (ter)

Quand on port'ra en terre,
C'drôl'de mironton mirontaine,
On grav'ra dans la pierre
L'épitaph' que voici : (ter)

« Churchill partait en guerre,
Ses alliés devant lui derrière
Vous avez fait "sa" guerre,
Ne l'oubliez jamais ! »

G. MAZEYRIE, IMP. ÉDITEUR, PARIS

Vichy French poster, c1942

In this remarkable Vichy poster, a pictorial history of the life of Winston Churchill drawn in the style of the famous Epinal tableaux, we see in Frame 1 Churchill's ancestor, the Duke of Marlborough, boldly striding into battle. By comparison, Winston is bombed out at home, gets his feet wet in the Norwegian campaign and becomes a hero in France 'by the skin of others.' Line 2 shows the British aptitude for championship sprinting in retreat and betraying their allies at Mers-el-Kebir and Dakar. In Line 3 Churchill invades the Balkans using the Serbs as a shield, leaves the Greeks stranded and marches backwards through Cyrenaica in North Africa. Line 4 shows the displeasure of his allies as Winston walks off the scene and is finally buried. His memorial bust has the epitaph: 'Churchill wages war, his allies in front, himself behind; you have fought *his* war – don't ever forget it!'

135

Deutscher Herbst 1944
Th Th Heine, 1944

The sands of time were running out for Hitler by the autumn of 1944. In 'German Autumn, 1944' the German Th Th Heine, exiled in Stockholm, shows Death shaking down swastikas like falling leaves as, behind, Germany burns (*left*). Kem's 'Hitler's nightmare' (*bottom*) makes a nice contrast to Buriko's hallucinating Churchill (*center*) produced earlier in *Il 420* (note swastika-legged cat). Kem's cartoon was so popular that it was reproduced in 126 different periodicals.

Churchill sees swastikas everywhere
Churchill: 'Hell! I must have had a drop too much tonight. This cross is really my cross.'
Buriko, *Il 420*, 4 August 1940

Hitler's nightmare
Kem, *Le Petit Parisien*, 6 April 1944

Jon's 'Two Types' were a great favorite among the Eighth Army, both in North Africa and later Italy, and became firmly established as comic characters in the minds of the military and civilian population. Indeed, General Freyberg once said that by themselves they were worth a division of troops. Both officers wear totally non-regulation clothes, apparently unsuitable for desert use but on closer examination highly rational: the neck-scarves serve to cover the face in sandstorms, the loose clothing, like a Bedouin's flapping robes, keeps the air circulating, and soft corduroy trousers are essential with so much grit in the desert (apparently it is almost impossible to remove sand-stains from ordinary trousers).

Two officers have a quirky off-hand humor all their own, as they smoke 'V2' cigarettes and season their meals with a sand-shaker.

W J P Jones (alias 'Jon') was born in Wales in 1914 and worked in advertising before joining the army. The first 'Two Types' cartoon appeared in *Eighth Army News* on 16 August 1944 and was later syndicated elsewhere. A 'demobbed' version of the series did not survive long, but Jon's 'Sporting Types' pocket cartoon was a long-running feature of the *Daily Mail* after the war.

'Last saw those two at El Agheila'
Jon, *Eighth Army News*, 1944

'Careful, careful, old man, it'll mean sending to Cairo for a new pair'
Jon, *Eighth Army News*, 1944

1945

Though the year of final Allied victory and the cessation of hostilities, 1945 was none the less perhaps the most horrific, in terms of human suffering, of all the years of the conflict. After the ghastly firestorms caused by Allied bombing raids on Dresden, crowded with refugees from the Eastern Front, in February, and the horrendous destruction visited upon the population of Tokyo the following month, there came the liberation of the concentration camps in April with their unbelievable statistics of mass murder and their desperate, emaciated survivors.

On the islands of Iwo Jima and Okinawa the Japanese fought fanatically against nearly half a million Allied troops and the German Home Guard (or *Volkssturm*) engaged in a desperate battle alongside the remains of the German Army following the encirclement of Berlin. By the end of May Mussolini had been executed by partisans, Hitler had committed suicide and Germany had surrendered to the Allies unconditionally.

But the final horror was yet to come. On 6 and 9 August 1945 a new kind of weapon, based not on chemical high explosives but on the principle of nuclear fission, was detonated above the Japanese towns of Hiroshima and Nagasaki. The loss of life – though less than that suffered in the Tokyo firestorm – was colossal, as was the power the weapon's secret held for the future.

The destruction of Hiroshima and Nagasaki and a simultaneous massive attack by the Soviet Union on Japanese forces in China led to Japan's final surrender and the end of World War II.

Hitler and Hirohito look on apprehensively as the confident Allied leaders (including Chiang Kai-shek) greet the New Year. Joseph Parrish was born in Tennessee in 1905 and worked for the *Chicago Tribune* from 1936 until he retired in 1972.

Destiny's child
Joseph Parrish, *Chicago Tribune*, 2 January 1945

R Tahir, *Akbaba* (cover), Istanbul, 10 June 1943

Çin işi, Japon işi!

Variation on the Japanese flag
Adolf Hoffmeister, *Jesters in Earnest*, London, 1943

Daniel Fitzpatrick, *St Louis Post-Dispatch*, 13 April 1945

President Roosevelt died on 12 April 1945, thus denied the 'final garland of victory.' The cartoonists paid their respects: in Fitzpatrick's cartoon the Stars and Stripes hanging at half-mast embraces the world while Low has an American GI presenting the laurels of victory to the president's empty desk in the White House.

Top: Two views of Japan's increasingly difficult position at this time. *Banzai*, meaning '10,000 years of life (to you),' was used as a salute to the emperor and also as a war cry by troops going into battle.

Last tribute
David Low, *Evening Standard*, 16 April 1945

Call from Hell: 'Do stop looking for Hitler. He's here all right, but we'd be glad to get rid of him. He's always making speeches and wants to reorganize this place on the model of Belsen'
Th Th Heine, 1946

In January 1945 the Red Army was in Warsaw while Hungary sought an armistice. By 5 March the United States First Army had entered Cologne and American troops crossed the Rhine at Remagen two days later. Vienna fell to the Soviet forces on 13 April and by 2 May Berlin was in Russian hands. The Nazis' number was definitely up but the mystery remained, where was Hitler? His disappearance led to considerable speculation, as the cartoon by Giles suggests. Th Th Heine had his own views, but in reality he had gone to ground in the *Führerbunker* in Berlin. Here he had married his long-time mistress, Eva Braun, and then committed suicide on 30 April 1945.

'Hey Joe – Do you see what I see?'
Carl Giles, *Daily Express*, 15 March 1945

'Here you are! Don't lose it again!'
Philip Zec, *Daily Mirror*, 8 May 1945

On 7 May 1945, Admiral Friedeburg and General Jodl (chiefs of the German Navy and Army, respectively) signed the unconditional surrender of the German forces at General Eisenhower's headquarters at Rheims, hostilities to cease officially at 2301 hours the following day. Thus on 8 May the British and Americans celebrated VE (Victory in Europe) Day. The Russians celebrated on the 9th. The Allies' sense of relief is well expressed in this powerful cartoon by Philip Zec.

Fougasse, British poster series, c1940

K Wieschala, German leaflet, c1940

With the secret police, spies and resistance fighters active throughout Europe, and the possibility of fifth columnists working in the unoccupied countries, the danger of vital information getting into the wrong hands was a constant concern for governments on both sides in the war. Perhaps the most famous cartoons on this subject are those in the series 'Careless Talk Costs Lives' (*above*), drawn as posters for the British Ministry of Information and depicting Hitler and his henchmen listening in to conversations. The United States and Italy produced posters on a similar theme and the leaflet by Wieschala (*left*) proves that the Germans were also anxious about the problem. The caption reads: 'What you say is no doubt important, but it's not for a stranger's ears.'

Right: Another *Collier*'s cover from the remarkable Arthur Szyk.

Arthur Szyk, *Collier's* (cover), 27 February 1943

SEAC
Bernard Partridge, *Punch*, 24 January 1945

The war in the Pacific and Far East continued to go the Allies' way at the beginning of 1945. The Burma Road was reopened on 23 January, allowing supplies and reinforcements to reach Chiang Kai-shek in China by the only land route, and the capture in March of Mandalay in Burma turned the tide against Japan. The image of Anglo-American flying-fish hovering over Mandalay in Partridge's drawing (*left*) is an appropriate choice, as air support from the RAF and USAAF played a decisive part in the war in this theatre. 'SEAC' stands for South East Asia Command.

Regular fire-bomb attacks on the Japanese home islands also continued. Tokyo was particularly badly hit, with 120,000 civilians being killed in one attack in March 1945. The American advance through the Philippines, though meeting with stern resistance, progressed slowly, island by island. The fighting on Iwo Jima was particularly heated – of the Japanese garrison of 20,000 only 216 were taken prisoner. The invasion of Okinawa on 1 April proved to be the biggest operation in the Pacific War. It also produced mass *kamikaze* attacks on the Allied Fleet. However, after a bitter struggle, the island was won in June.

The plight of the Japanese is well summed up in the two cartoons below.

**'But we still hold the initiative –
we can surrender any time we want'**
M Bernstein, *PM*, 1945

'Ah! Those were the good old days!'
New York Times, August 1945

'Baby play with nice ball?'
David Low, *Evening Standard*, 9 August 1945

Surrender – including face
David Low, *Evening Standard*, 11 August 1945

The first atomic bomb was dropped on Hiroshima, Japan's seventh largest city, on 6 August 1945. A single American B-29 Superfortress, the 'Enola Gay' flown by Colonel Paul Tibbetts, released a parachute-borne charge that was detonated above the city. In a few seconds 78,000 people lay dead and 40,000 injured (with many more dying of radiation exposure later) and every building in a three-mile radius from the explosion was flattened. Three days later a further bomb – this time made of plutonium rather than uranium – was dropped on the port of Nagasaki, killing around 40,000 people. At about the same time the Soviet Union declared war on Japan. In a massive assault, 1,500,000 men attacked the Japanese Army in Manchuria, smashing through their defenses instantly and threatening the enemy homeland from the west. On the 15th the God-Emperor Hirohito broadcast to the masses that Japan was to surrender. Low's cartoons sum up the situation while hinting at future dangers.

Saul Steinberg, *New Yorker*

Hermann Goering (1893-1946) had been a member of Baron von Richthofen's 'Flying Circus' in World War I and had himself shot down 22 aircraft. He became *Reichsmarschall* and Hitler's official successor in 1939 and was the head of the Luftwaffe. However, after the Battle of Britain and Stalingrad (where he had failed to deliver promised supplies by air to Paulus's beleaguered Sixth Army), his power waned. He began to live in a dream world, a tendency increased by his use of drugs such as morphine, to which he had become addicted. He also took great delight in flamboyant non-regulation uniforms, as these three cartoons illustrate. Saul Steinberg (1914-99) was born in Rumania and studied architecture in Milan (where he also contributed cartoons to *Bertoldo*) before being forced to leave Italy in 1941. After a period in the Dominican Republic he finally settled in the United States, was naturalized and served in the US Navy until 1945. His work for the *New Yorker*, *Liberty* and other magazines earned him considerable renown.

'It's for the Braemar Games – like it?'
Nicolas Bentley, *Animal, Vegetable and South Kensington*, London, 1940

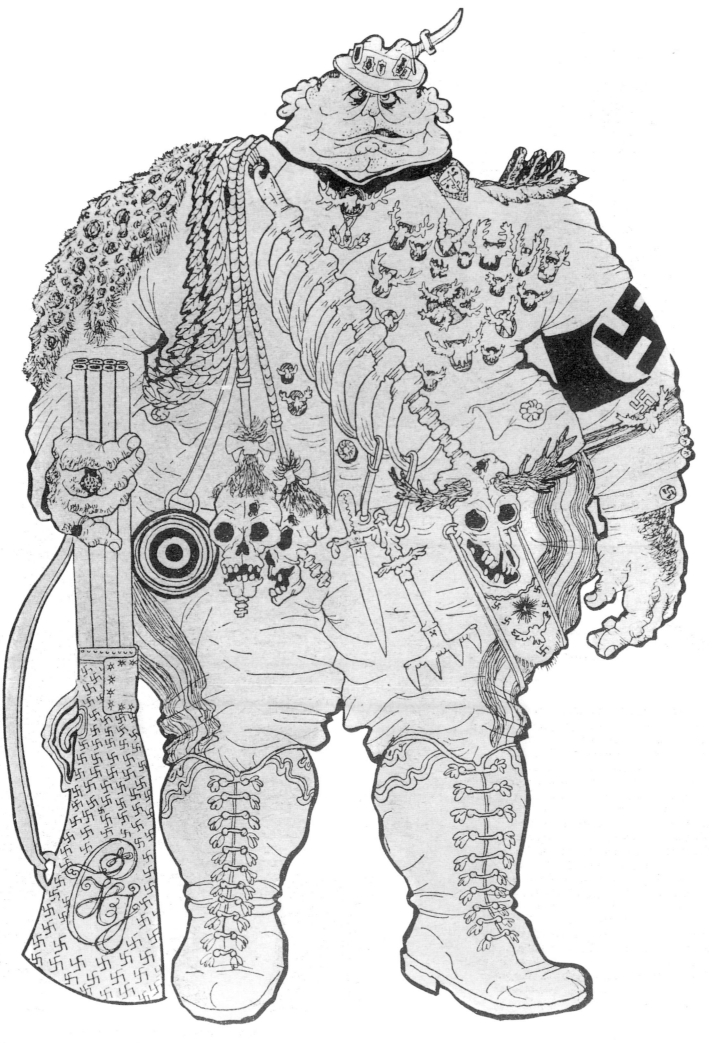

Bert, *Das III Reich in der Karikatur* Prague, 1934

'Fresh, spirited American troops, flushed with victory,
are bringing in thousands of hungry,
ragged, battle-weary prisoners' (News item)
Bill Mauldin, 1944

'Just gimme a coupla Aspirin. I already got a Purple Heart'
Bill Mauldin, 1944

Three cartoons by Bill Mauldin (b. 1921) from his 'Up Front' series beloved of the GIs. The series began in 1940 and first appeared in *45th Division News*, becoming progressively more powerful as Mauldin himself began to see action in the invasion of Sicily. It also began to be syndicated in the official United States Army daily newspaper, *Stars and Stripes* (whose staff Mauldin joined in 1943) and the weekly *Yank*. Willie and Joe continued for a while into peacetime, but eventually faded out except for a brief reappearance during the Korean War. The three cartoons shown here are perhaps the most reproduced of all his drawings, and 'Fresh, spirited American troops . . .' won him a Pulitzer Prize in 1945. (A 'Purple Heart' was a decoration awarded to members of the American forces for a wound incurred in action.)

Bill Mauldin, 1944

Private Breger, who achieved international fame in the 'GI Joe' strip for the Mediterranean edition of the US forces daily newspaper, *Stars and Stripes*, and the weekly *Yank*, was the creation of Sergeant (later Lieutenant) Dave Breger. These three drawings, which give a good sample of the character's activities, are taken from a collection published in Britain in 1944. The freckle-faced, bespectacled soldier first appeared in the *Saturday Evening Post* on 30 August 1941 as 'Private Breger,' but when *Yank* took up the character his name was changed to 'GI Joe' for copyright reasons. A civilian version, 'Mr Breger,' was syndicated after the war until 22 March 1970.

'And with the luminous paint he figures enemy night raiders will fly right into it!'

Dave Breger, *Private Breger in Britain*, London, 1944

'I don't care if you ARE from Chicago! Take your gun outta that violin case!'

Dave Breger, *Private Breger in Britain*, London, 1944

'I'll be right back. I forgot my identification tags!'

Dave Breger, *Private Breger in Britain*, London, 1944

Popular Misconceptions (in Germany) – The English
Pont, *Punch*, 24 January 1940

The English Europe-puzzle
Signal, December 1940

Pont's perceptive jokes are not so far from the truth as one would like to believe. That the Germans under the sway of Hitler's theory of the *Herrenvolk* and the new Aryanism saw themselves as flaxen-haired incarnations of the heroes of Asgard and the characters in the *Nibelungenlied* (*left*) is emphasized by the popularity of Wagner's 'Ring' cycle in the 1930s and 1940s. And, like it or not, the image of the British as monocled war-mongering Hooray Henrys and Harriets dressed in plus-fours and sensible tweeds has long been prevalent outside the United Kingdom. The example (*above*) from the Nazi illustrated magazine, *Signal*, is a typical example.

Popular Misconceptions (in Germany) – The Germans
Pont, *Punch*, 14 February 1940

MGM, *The Blitz Wolf*, 1942

Animated films and indeed the 'stars' of prewar animated shorts and features were much in evidence during the conflict and were used for both propaganda and training purposes. The Disney studio turned out films with titles such as *Donald Gets Drafted*, *Victory through Air Power* and *Out of the Frying Pan into the Firing Line*, and even won an Academy Award for the Donald Duck short *Der Führer's Face* (1942), beating the equally brilliant *The Blitz Wolf* by Tex Avery – the first cartoon ever released by MGM – by a short head. (Avery had ended his liaison with Warner Brothers immediately before this with a Bugs Bunny film set in the Pacific theatre, *Crazy Convoy*.) Britain, Russia, Japan and Germany also produced excellent animated films at this time, a particularly notable UK effort being *Dustbin Parade* (1942) created for the Ministry of Information by Halas and Batchelor.

Walt Disney Productions, *Donald Gets Drafted*, 1942

'Even if their War Crimes Commission does let us go free after the war, Himmler – I can't imagine you settling down in a little grocery business or something'

Carl Giles, *Sunday Express*, 1945

Tout s'explique!
'Mais si ! Je jouais double-jeu quand je faisais croire que je jouais double-jeu!'

J Sennep, 1945

Witnesses for the prosecution
Daniel Fitzpatrick, *St Louis Post-Dispatch*, 30 April 1945

In January and October 1942, meetings of Allied representatives declared that Axis war criminals would be punished by a United Nations commission after the war. A major factor in the prosecution in 1945-46 was the horrific evidence of the Nazis' treatment of the Jews and others in the Concentration Camps. Twenty-one Nazis stood trial at Nuremberg in Bavaria (scene of the huge annual Nazi rallies), including Goering, Hess, Ribbentrop and Doenitz – Hitler, Goebbels and Himmler having already committed suicide. A similar court was held in Tokyo to try Japanese leaders for the maltreatment of Allied prisoners and other breaches of the Geneva Convention. Twenty-eight men stood in the dock there, including Tojo but not Emperor Hirohito. Other nations held their own trials: Quisling was executed in Norway, Mussolini had been murdered by partisans earlier, Antonescu was executed in Rumania and Laval in France. Pétain was sentenced to life imprisonment, although he claimed in his defense that he had been playing a double game all along. Sennep's cartoon 'All is explained!' comments on this less than convincing claim. The caption reads: 'But yes! I was playing a double game when I made out I was playing a double game!'

The last line of Fascist defense
Kukryniksi, 1945

David Low and the Kukryniksi group (along with other cartoonists, such as Flatter) attended the Nuremberg trials as official artists. In his *Nuremberg Sketchbook* series, Low caricatures various Nazi leaders. Of these, Ribbentrop, Streicher, Frank, Sauckel and Jodl were executed, Goering committed suicide in his cell and the rest received long prison sentences, except Schacht, who was acquitted. The Kukryniksi group also catch the mood of the trials (left), with sombre Nazis defended by an army of lawyers using pens, paper and legal niceties instead of guns.

LOW'S NUEREMBERG SKETCHBOOK — № 1

LOW'S NUREMBERG SKETCHBOOK – Nº 2

LOW'S NUREMBERG SKETCHBOOK – Nº 3

'Be funny if the siren went now, wouldn't it?'
Carl Giles, *Sunday Express*, 19 August 1945

After the unconditional surrender of Japan there was considerable festivity amongst the conquering powers. Giles's wild street-scene gives an impression of how Londoners reacted to the news (though note the bored-looking group near the policemen). VJ-Day and the end of World War II were officially celebrated on 2 September.

Unter den Linden
Daniel Fitzpatrick, *St Louis Post-Dispatch*, 30 January 1945

The immediate aftermath of the war is well portrayed in these two cartoons. Sillince compares the scene confronting the liberating Allied soldiers in Europe with that experienced after World War I. Fitzpatrick's spectral German soldier, the Iron Cross at his neck, salutes an imaginary Hitler in a devastated Unter den Linden – all that is left of the great Berlin thoroughfare where the Nazi armies once paraded before their Führer.

'The old place hasn't changed a bit from 1917!'
W A Sillince, *Punch*, 10 January 1945

Right: A view of the Allied victory, published before Roosevelt's death in April. (He was succeeded by his vice-president, Harry S Truman.)

'And how are we feeling today?'
Bernard Partridge, *Punch*, 21 February 1945

In Kem's Christmas card of the post-war world (*below*), President Truman of the United States – in the guise of the Statue of Liberty – holds both physical and monetary power. With the secret of the atom bomb in America's control and the world's financial base transferred to the dollar following the Bretton Woods conference in 1944, all the major Allied nations want to be friends with her – or do they? Stalin, Attlee, De Gaulle and Chiang Kai-shek all hold out hands of friendship, but they are really reaching for the Bomb . . .

Kem, Christmas card, December 1945

INDEX

Acknowledgments

The Publisher has made every effort to trace the copyright owners for the cartoons reproduced in this book. Advice on omissions would be greatly appreciated and will be included in future editions. The Author and Publisher would like to acknowledge and thank the following institutions, companies and individuals for the cartoons as listed below:

Archiv Gerstenberg, pages: 30(top), 32, 42(left), 82(left), 128(bottom right),/New York Times © 1945 144(bottom right)
Arthur Barker Ltd/Weidenfeld, page: 78(bottom)
Bison Books, page: 150(top right)
British Library, pages: 28(bottom left), 79(bottom), 86(top left), 93(both), 101(bottom right), 115(bottom), 131(bottom left)
Co-operative Press, pages: 56(top left), 108(both), 109(both)

© Chatto & Windus, page: 52(bottom)
© DACS, 1989, pages: 114(top & bottom left), 129(middle), 134(bottom), 136(top), 144(top), 152(bottom)
Express News & Feature Service, pages: 29(top), 30(bottom), 40(top), 48(bottom right), 58(top), 65(top), 81(top), 126(bottom), 140(bottom), 152(top), 156
G William Ganagan Collection, Hoover Institution Archives, page: 83(top)
Herald & Weekly Times/Melbourne Argus, pages: 28(top), 31(top), 54(top left), 88(top right)
Robert Hunt Library, page: 131(bottom right)
Illustrated London News, pages: 29(bottom), 101(top left)
Collection of the Imperial War Museum/Joseph Flatter: 20(left),/Jiscenko: 102(both), 103,/William Hooper 113(bottom),/Ronald Searle: 128(top),/Milos Zubac: 128(bottom left),/Mastrick: 135(top), W.J.P Jones: 137(both)
Trustees of the Imperial War Museum, pages: 14(top), 33(left), 35, 42(right), 46(top), 67, 70, 71(top), 75, 79(top), 83(bottom), 87(left), 90(top right & bottom), 91(both), 97(bottom), 112(bottom), 116(top right & bottom two), 120(top), 131(top), 142(both top)
© IPC Magazines, pages: 34(bottom), 100
Estate of Osbert Lancaster by permission of John Murray Publishers, pages: 41(right), 51(bottom left), 80(top left), 85(top middle & right), 101(top right), 104(bottom)
© 1989 Lorne Harvey Productions. All rights reserved. Used with permission, page: 94
Courtesy Macmillan, Inc./Lawson Wood: 34(right),/Arthur Szyk: 71(bottom), 74, 143
Mail Newspapers PLC/SOLO Syndication,/Daily Sketch, pages: 61(left),/Evening News, pages: 26(bottom), 36(both), 56(top right), 107(bottom),/Evening Standard, pages: 12(top), 16(bottom), 25(top), 40(Bottom), 41(left), 44(bottom), 45(top), 47(bottom), 50(both), 58(top left), 63(both), 65(bottom), 66(top), 68(bottom), 84(bottom), 86(bottom), 88(bottom), 126(top), 127(both), 129(bottom right), 139(bottom right), 145(bottom both), 154(bottom), 155(both),/News Chronicle, pages: 25, 72(bottom), 126(middle), 129(top)
Estate of Kimon Marengo/Alex Marengo, pages: 11(bottom), 66(bottom right), 105(bottom), 117(both), 136(bottom), 158(bottom)
© Bill Mauldin, pages: 119(both top), 148(all three)
Mirror Group Newspapers/Daily Herald, pages: 11(top left), 23,/Daily Mirror, pages: 44(top left), 57(bottom), 97(top), 106(all three), 141,/Sunday Pictorial, pages: 66(bottom left), 89(bottom right), 92(bottom left), 110(top), 122(bottom)
Louis Mitelberg (Tim), page: 48(bottom)
Morning Star, page: 81(bottom)
Frederick Muller Ltd, pages: 95(top two), 133(both)
John Murray Publishers Ltd, pages: 66(top), 86(top right), 92(top), 105(top), 134(top), 139(top right)
Museo Civico L'Bailo, pages: 56(bottom right), 90(top left)
New York News, Inc, reprinted with permission, page: 17(top)
New Yorker, pages: 60(top right), 62(bottom), 76(left), 89(top), 110(bottom), 146(top)
Newark Evening News, pages: 123(bottom)
Peter Newark's Military Pictures, page: 85(bottom)
Reprinted by permission of the Putnam Publishing Group from the New Order by Arthur Szyk. © 1941 Arthur Szyk, pages: 47(top), 114(bottom right)
Quadrant, page: 80(top right)
Punch Archive, pages: 26(top), 27(top), 33(top & bottom right), 37(bottom), 41(top), 48(top), 49(bottom), 51(top), 53(bottom & top left), 54(bottom), 56(bottom), 58(bottom), 59(all three), 60(bottom), 64(top), 95(bottom), 96(all three), 107(top), 121, 122(top), 132(bottom), 144(top), 146(bottom), 150(both), 157(top)
St. Louis Post-Dispatch, pages: 16(top right), 46(bottom left), 89(bottom left), 92(bottom right), 139(bottom left), 153, 157(top)
SCRUSSR, pages: 101(bottom left), 154(top)
Ronald Searle/Tessa Sayle Agency, page: 53(top left)
Turner Entertainment, page: 151(top)
© 1942 Loew's Inc. Ren. 1969 Metro-Goldwyn-Mayer Inc.
Tribune Media Services, reprinted by permission, page: 23(top), 138
US Air Force Photo Collection, NASM, page: 98(right)
© Walt Disney Company, page: 151(bottom)
Washington Star, page: 24
Wiener Library, pages: 18, 19, 20(top & bottom right), 22, 31, 43(both), 44(top right), 51(bottom right), 54(top right), 55, 57(top), 61(right), 64(bottom), 69, 77(bottom), 84(top both), 87(right), 88(top left), 98(left), 120(bottom both), 132(top), 142(bottom), 147

Special thanks to Michael Foot for permission to quote material from *Loyalists and Loners*, Collins, 1986.